SOAR!

ALSO BY T. D. JAKES

SOAR!

Build Your Vision
from the Ground Up

T. D. JAKES

New York   Nashville

Copyright © 2017 by TDJ Enterprises, LLP

Cover design by Jason Scuderi
Cover photography by Martin Adolfsson

FaithWords
Hachette Book Group
1290 Avenue of the Americas, New York, NY 10104
faithwords.com
twitter.com/faithwords

First Edition: October 2017 10\17

FaithWords is a division of Hachette Book Group, Inc. The FaithWords name and logo are trademarks of Hachette Book Group, Inc.

The publisher is not responsible for websites (or their content) that are not owned by the publisher.

The Hachette Speakers Bureau provides a wide range of authors for speaking events. To find out more, go to www.hachettespeakersbureau.com or call (866) 376-6591.

Unless otherwise noted Scriptures are taken from the *Holy Bible, New International Version*®, NIV®, Copyright © 1973, 1978, 1984, 2011 by Biblica, Inc.® Used by permission. All rights reserved worldwide.

Scripture quotations marked (ESV) are from the ESV® Bible (*The Holy Bible, English Standard Version*®), copyright © 2001 by Crossway, a publishing ministry of Good News Publishers. Used by permission. All rights reserved.

Scriptures marked (KJV) are taken from the *King James Version of the Bible*.

Scripture quotations marked (NASB) are taken from the *New American Standard Bible*®, Copyright © 1960, 1962, 1963, 1968, 1971, 1972, 1973, 1975, 1977, 1995 by The Lockman Foundation. Used by permission.

Scripture quotations marked (NKJV) are taken from the *New King James Version*®. Copyright © 1982 by Thomas Nelson. Used by permission. All rights reserved.

Scripture quotations marked (WEB) are taken from the *World English Bible*.

Library of Congress Control Number: 2017945957

ISBN: 978-1-4555-5390-7 (hardcover), 978-1-4555-5388-4 (ebook), 978-1-4555-8404-8 (international trade), 978-1-4555-8219-8 (large print), 978-1-5460-2716-4 (signed edition), 978-1-5460-2715-7 (B&N signed edition), 978-1-4789-4532-1 (South African trade)

Printed in the United States of America

LSC-C

10 9 8 7 6 5 4 3 2 1

To the more than ten thousand former inmates who have successfully graduated from our Texas Offenders Reentry Initiative. Your strength, determination, faith, and dedication exemplify what it means to build a new life and mount up on wings like eagles. May you continue to soar even as you inspire others to follow you across the sky!

Contents

Contents

PART IV
SOAR TO NEW HEIGHTS

SOAR!

Cleared for Takeoff!

If we worked on the assumption that what is accepted as true really is true, then there would be little hope for advance.

—Orville Wright

You never forget the first time you fly.

Racing down the runway in a huge metal cylinder with wings, you gasp as the plane surges and lifts and you realize that the two-ton machine you're in no longer touches the ground. Through the porthole window, you watch as the terminal, parking lot, trees, lawns, houses, parks, businesses, cars, and highways recede until they become as small as children's toys littering a quilt of gray, brown, and green.

Then you can no longer see what is beneath you as the plane climbs higher and higher into an expanse of blue embroidered with white. You smile to yourself as golden strands of sunlight filter through the clouds like giant hands fingering the endless silk of the sky. Your mind marvels at the fact you are thousands of feet in the air even as your stomach lurches to remind you it prefers the solid ground below.

The only sounds are the drowsy hum of the plane's engines and your own heartbeat drumming a rhythm of equal parts terror and exhilaration. You wonder if this is how a bird feels as it soars high above the earth, never looking back at the branch from which it departed, only ahead toward the distant horizon. You know you will never forget this experience and all its sensations of delight and wonder, anxiety and fear.

Perhaps your first flight was not as magical as my own, but I bet it was just as memorable. I was young, probably around eleven or twelve years old, and flew by myself from Charleston, West Virginia, to Cleveland, Ohio, where my father was receiving medical treatment for the kidney disease that would eventually claim his life. My mother was already there and would be the one to pick me up on arrival. Even my concern for my father's health could not dampen the thrill I experienced flying that first time as a child passenger.

That excitement had been ignited in me years earlier when my father would drive our family up the hill toward the airport for one of life's simple and absolutely free pleasures—watching the planes come and go. Summer days especially we would drive up and park where we had an optimal view of the Cessna jets with their wealthy business travelers as well as the commercial 747s shuttling assorted passengers through the friendly skies. The red-orange sun would be descending in the afternoon sky, heavy from the weight of its own sweltering heat, and we'd have all the windows rolled down to catch a breeze as my siblings and I laughed and pointed out specific clouds to each other—a camel, a roller coaster, the face of one of our aunties—while waiting for the next plane to land or take off.

We couldn't afford the trips to the Florida beaches or vacations to the Grand Canyon that my classmates would boast about the rest of the summer. But we had the next best thing, stimulating our imaginations more than any visit to Disneyland, driving up that hill by the airport before or sometimes after dinner from time to time. As we sat in the car or ventured out on the lot to get a closer look, we would imagine we were on those planes, going God knows where, to see God knows what!

Defying Gravity

Flying for the first time is a lot like creating your own business, launching a start-up, or establishing a nonprofit organization. Undertaking such ventures requires overcoming the inherent fear of leaving the safety of solid ground behind, defying gravity, and embarking on a journey of unexpected variables within predictable patterns toward a deliberate destination. In other words, both require a little bit of crazy and a whole lot of courage!

Sitting there as a kid and watching planes fly in and out, I loved listening to my parents tell us how their parents grew up during a time when all they could see in the sky were birds and clouds, occupying space where people could not go. My mother was born in 1926, and while I'm not sure when her mother was born, I suspect it was around the time the Wright brothers first successfully launched their fixed-wing aircraft at Kitty Hawk, North Carolina, in 1903. Why do I suspect this? Because my great-aunts were afraid of flying until they died!

I wasn't afraid so much as I was curious. Even as a kid, I couldn't help but wonder what Orville and Wilbur Wright must have had on their minds and in their hearts that caused them to build a machine heavy enough to hold human beings and yet light enough to fly through the air. What compelled them to utilize scrap materials from a bicycle shop to build wings that would forever change the world? What drove them to try and fail and try some more and to keep trying time and time again even when the wind was against them? Whatever it was, their passionate pursuit of innovation transformed inspiration and perspiration into aviation!

The Wright brothers knew the laws of gravity worked against them. They knew that people thought they were crazy for even trying to create a flying machine that could soar through the skies above everyone else. However, they defied the odds—and gravity—by refusing to give up until they discovered new laws, principles of aerodynamics that enabled a craft of a certain weight traveling at a certain velocity to gain momentum and catch flight. These pioneers of the skies created a new normal, a paradigm shift so life-changing that it transformed the way we travel, transact business, and conduct warfare.

Now maybe you aren't interested in building a flying machine. But in essence the Wright brothers' endeavor is the goal of every entrepreneur. What do you need to build in order to get up there into the sky of economic viability? How can you take what you have and escape the gravitational pull of a salary that limits your ability to escape from living paycheck to paycheck?

At the end of the day, the same innovative, relentless tenacity that fueled the Wright brothers determines the direction of your own dreams. It is the power of one transformative belief held firmly in place, the daring idea that says just because I haven't seen it modeled in my past doesn't mean that I cannot create something that changes the trajectory of my future. Simply put, it is the power to make the seemingly impossible become your new reality.

When I stood in the parking lot watching the planes soar all those years ago, I wondered if I would ever travel beyond the confines into which I was born by embarking on a flight that would carry me off to new, exciting adventures and a life defined by limitless possibility.

Could I create my own flying machine that would enable me to soar into a future with more options and opportunities than the ground beneath my feet presently offered? Standing out there as a boy I knew that someday, some way, my personal vision of what I could do would become a reality. I would build something that would transport me beyond where I stood into the place where I, too, could mount up on eagle's wings with the help of the Lord.

I knew I could build my vision from the ground up and find the power to make it *soar*, and that has made all the difference!

Get Your Vision Off the Ground

You, too, hold within your hands the power to soar.

You may not have known it and believed it at an early age like I did, but it remains true nonetheless. You don't have angel wings sprouting from your shoulder blades, possess superpowers like many heroes on our movie screens, or own a Cessna aircraft, but if you have the desire for advancement in your life and you're willing to risk the familiar comfort of where you are for the adrenaline-fueled thrill of where you want to be, then you can fly. Flight is possible even for those who are emotionally, financially, and creatively fatigued. You can take your vision, build it into something remarkable, and reach heights you could have never imagined.

If you doubt my faith in such flight for your own life, then consider the wind—invisible yet powerful enough to level buildings. Even as it provides lift for planes weighing thousands of pounds, wind has no color, no texture, no visible shape, and no sentient intentionality. As a force of nature, wind is easier to document by its external effects than by its inherent attributes.

Likewise for a person rising from where they are to where they want to be: their ascendancy on the outside must begin with the transcendence of a personal vision for what they can be on the inside. As surely as wind moves a 747, a change in your life's perspective cannot always be conveyed adequately by language. But its effect could have immediate as well as generational consequences on your ability to reach new heights beyond your present wingspan.

And that's what this book is all about.

I will share many tips as we prepare for this journey. My hope is that they will be valuable whether you are new to this whole entrepreneurial process or whether you are a venerable veteran of catapulting new endeavors into the wild blue yonder. I do not know everything about being a successful entrepreneur, but what I do know I humbly offer you within these pages. Your business plan—whether conceptual or concrete—will serve as your flight manual for getting your vision off the ground and sustaining a successful flight toward a divine destination beyond your imagination.

From the Control Tower

Years ago, when I was much younger, I worked for the now defunct Piedmont Airlines in the baggage claim area. It was merely a summer job, but after my early years of gazing at planes from the parking lot, I got a much closer look at how they operated. I quickly learned that a landing plane receives directions and guidance from the ground crew. Waving a brightly colored flag or illuminated baton, these team members guided the pilot to park the plane at a specific gate or in another area designated for passengers and baggage to be unloaded.

Learning these signs was requisite for any full-time airline employee working on the tarmac, and obviously the pilots had to understand what the signals meant in order to comply. But I also recognized that when it was time for a plane to take off, no such ground signals were available or implemented. All direction came from the lofty pinnacle of the control tower tasked with navigating the pilot through the maze of other flights taking off and landing. The pilot received directions transmitted by a voice within his headset. No matter how experienced the pilot may have been, he was unable to see all the other aircraft lurking in the clouds, circling the airport, or preparing to land. This kind of guidance was given by the informed person in the tower, someone with the ability to take into consideration comprehensive information that wasn't just privileged but was also critical to increase safety and to avoid calamities.

Like a veteran air traffic controller, I want to do the same for you. I want to help you avoid the dangerous liability of not clearly seeing information that could drastically change the outcome of your smooth takeoff into unknown skies. Here are a few tips that are designed for the benefit of increasing the likelihood of success and to diminish the likelihood of casualties and collateral damage associated with getting your new venture off the ground. From my perch of many decades of living, working, and thriving as an entrepreneur, I hope to provide some vital information to help you gain velocity as well as offer directive guidance for avoiding potential disasters that could cause you to crash.

A Bird's-Eye View

There is no easy formula for entrepreneurial success, for part of the joy inherent in flight is building your own wings from scratch and discovering new destinations. But over the years I've identified an adaptable and progressive process that will focus your energies in the most productive ways for the sustainable flight of your new venture. For the entrepreneur already airborne, I hope to introduce concepts that will enable you to become more stream-lined and to increase your momentum by decreasing the excess baggage impeding your ascent. Some steps in the process may be familiar while others may surprise you, but I can guarantee that all of them will challenge you, inspire you, and elevate you beyond ground level.

Here is a bird's-eye view of our journey together.

1. *CATCH A VISION OF YOUR DESTINATION*
   We will first explore how to turn your flights of fancy into fights you can win in the battle to get your vision off the ground. We'll discuss how to connect to your passion and how to identify your motives for wanting to soar as a new business owner, discovering along the way why the time has never been better for female entrepreneurs to take flight. Next, I will guide you in identifying a problem that intersects with your passion, because no matter how gifted and enthusiastic you may be, if there is no market for what you want to offer you're doomed to spin your wheels on an endless runway of frustrating futil-ity. Digging deeper into your desire to be an entrepreneur, we will examine the commitment required if your vision is to take flight.

2. *BUILD YOUR WINGS*
   Taking action to turn your dream into a flying machine requires a strategic flight plan and the resourcefulness to use the materials available to you. As with building a plane, most entrepreneurs start with pieces, parts, and potentials. Your proficiency at fusing these fragments creates the uniqueness of your brand and hastens your goal of operating at higher altitudes than your past experiences have propelled you. While

imitating those who have gone before you is crucial to your success, knowing how and when to innovate and blaze your own trail is just as vital. And if you're going to construct an aircraft capable of sustained flight, you need a flight crew of kindred spirits willing to build, bond, and board this new venture with you.

3. ***CLEAR THE CLOUDS***

Defying gravity and getting off the ground is only the first step in sustaining a long, smooth flight for your new business. Understand that between liftoff and stability, you will experience a certain period of volatility that's inherent with growth. As you learn to anticipate turbulence as part of the process, you will discover that rough air is always an attribute of ascension. Your ability to anticipate that turbulence rather than be rattled by it is an important part of flight. Experience reveals that what may seem gut-wrenching at first is merely a sign that you're at a higher level. You can relax in the midst of those bumps and explore new routes both above and below your current altitude, where your business can enjoy smooth sailing. Learning early on from small mistakes often determines the difference between your business's ability to survive a crisis and the likelihood that it will crash.

4. ***SOAR TO NEW HEIGHTS***

Thriving and growing frequently require adapting to new conditions, adjusting your flight plan, and even changing course for a new destination. While refueling your engines and maintaining the body of your business may seem obvious, you may be surprised how many new ventures fail in their first year because of easily avoidable mistakes and misperceptions. No matter your venture's focus, once it's airborne you can break the barriers beyond previous possibilities if you're boldly willing to go where no one has gone before.

Kiss the Clouds

Whatever your business may be, it will never work if you can't get it off the ground and into the air. It is my hope that I can share tips and tools with you that will help you build the internal fortitude necessary to get your dream off the runway and into the air. Guiding and assisting you to the best of my ability, I want you to experience the exhilaration that comes only from watching something you've created from scratch catch the winds and trends of sustainable flight. There's no greater, more satisfying feeling in the world than giving birth to a dream with strong wings.

If you've never done this or if you have done it many times before, you know there are risks involved. But with any endeavor of value, risk is requisite for reaping rewards. Yes, there will be a wave of anxious fear, which is a healthy caution. Just imagine what the Wright brothers must have felt as their craft left the ground and kissed the clouds! Surely it was a heart-racing, head-spinning moment of jubilation unlike any other. And you can feel it, too—that thrill experienced by every visionary when their abstract ideals and figurative fantasies materialize and take flight.

So buckle up and fasten your seat belt because objects and ideas overhead are definitely about to shift! Whether you are twenty-six or sixty-six, this feeling of liftoff makes the hair on your head or the sweat on your bald spot tingle! Already you can start to feel yourself break away from the gravitational pull that keeps gazers on the ground. Your feet are itching to rise into the air and ascend as you make your vision a reality! This is the pivotal moment of decision that creates the exhilaration of entrepreneurs, a high that is beyond anything you've ever experienced.

Are you ready? Are you willing to leave the safety of where you stand now in order to soar in the limitless skies above? Then turn the page, my entrepreneurial friend, and let's get started—you have been cleared for takeoff!

PART I

EXPAND YOUR VISION

Hope deferred makes the heart sick, but a longing fulfilled is a tree of life.

—Proverbs 13:12

CHAPTER 1

Ignite Your Flight

Putting Vision in Motion

Flight without feathers is not easy.
—Plautus

People frequently ask me, "Bishop Jakes, how do you do all the things you do? How do you juggle your ministry with speaking, filming, producing, recording, and writing?" Typically, these questions are followed by further interrogation about the various diverse endeavors that consume my energies and how others can similarly turn their passions into possibilities as well. While there's no one-size-fits-all answer, I love to address these questions because my answers can be found in the way I see the world and my role in it. Simply put, I consider myself an entrepreneur, although that is the "high cotton" term, as my grandmother would say.

In fact, I come from a family of entrepreneurs, but we never used that word to describe ourselves. My father always said he was just trying to hustle and stay in the game, like everyone else. You may find the term *hustler* an irreverent way to describe my dear old dad, Ernest Jakes, but no other word comes to mind to convey his combination of boundless energy, desperate innovation, and relentless determination.

My father was a good man, hardworking and relentless. The vision for his life wasn't to be rich or famous. He considered such an aspiration too high for someone so low on life's proverbial totem pole. My father was hustling just so we could get by. He worked double shifts and weekends so that he and my mother could finally afford amenities like a doorbell, carpet in our living room, and maybe, if they could save up long enough, a garage where he could store his tools and protect his truck from the elements.

My father wasn't devoid of ambition, but it wasn't the driving force in his heart. He was a black man in the 1960s, raising a family in West Virginia, who didn't have time to think about what he could acquire beyond meeting our basic needs. He wasn't dreaming about shiny new Cadillacs or gold-plated bathroom fixtures. He was just trying to buy a house for his family that perhaps had more than one bathroom and maybe a bedroom for each of his three children. Those were his goals. They were simple and he was focused on providing for his family.

And in order to do that, he had to hustle.

Attitude Affects Altitude

When I was growing up and someone would ask me what my father did for a living, it was always a difficult question to answer. Because he did *everything*: he sold appliances and household items through a company called Service Wholesale. On weekends, he had another gig selling fresh fish shipped into town on the train. My mother, brother, sister, and I would weigh and wash the fish, then wrap each piece in newspaper before we packed the fish back into the boxes. Then my father drove around the neighborhood, going from house to house, selling the fish to neighbors for a minimal margin of profit.

Whether he was selling new cookware or fresh trout, my father's beat-up old red Ford pickup truck was his "distribution channel." That truck also served to get him to his other jobs, such as odd jobs for neighbors and cleaning up after hours for local businesses. Fortunately, in the process of working all those jobs, my father finally stumbled upon a business through which he was able to drop many of his side endeavors and focus on one primary enterprise.

He gradually went from being a jack-of-all-trades juggling many jobs to a singularly focused entrepreneur. We had others in our community who paved the way, a few black doctors and lawyers with their own practices. Those educated men had to hustle up their own business, too, but because they were educated, they knew there was more to business than just making the sale. They knew you had to be well rounded in business, providing the service as well as the management.

Looking back, I suspect they learned this lesson quickly, although my father never did. He didn't wield a college degree the way they did and never had a wealth of opportunities. What he did have was a mop, a bucket, a strong work ethic, creativity, and a can-do, never-quit attitude. With that, my father started a janitorial services business, beginning as a one-man operation cleaning office buildings.

My father scraped and scrambled in order to do all that needed doing—getting new customers, spreading the word about his business, and of course the actual cleaning itself. Over the years, he built his company to more than fifty employees, with janitorial contracts all over the state. He even had to get an office after a while and eventually hired a secretary, Greta, who had bright red hair.

Although his business was growing and he was providing for his family, my father was never able to break through to a higher level because of his mind-set. He got the wings of his vision off the ground, but he never left the low altitude of his I-have-to-do-it-all attitude. He struggled with managing his business and his employees because he ran it the same way he had when he was selling fish from the back of his old Ford truck. He was still out there talking up business instead of taking care of business. There was no one casting a bigger vision and looking at the larger picture, connecting the dots between the daily details and the distant destination. No one was minding the business of his busyness, making sure bookkeeping records were in order, bills were being paid, and customers were paying on time.

My father's vision was limited. He was able to build his flying machine and get it in the air.

But he didn't know how to help it soar.

Legacy of Love's Labor

My father came by his work ethic honestly, though. It was in his DNA because his mother, my grandmother, was herself a force to be reckoned with. It had been passed down to her through the generations because *her* grandmother had to pick cotton for slave masters just so she could survive. So she passed that do-whatever-it-takes drive on to her children.

And my father wasn't the only entrepreneur in our house. My mother was a teacher by day, but when she came home after work she took the little bit of money she and my dad had set aside and invested in real estate. She rented out small homes and apartments, collecting rent until the day she died. So, in our house, the entrepreneurial mind-set was a family heirloom passed down from generation to generation on both sides of the family.

That's how their entrepreneurial example, the legacy of their love's labor, was passed on to me. When I was growing up, however, I had no idea that my parents were setting examples that would influence my future. I didn't really know what was happening or realize how much I was absorbing from listening, watching, and contributing to their endeavors. But no one could have the kind of hustling work ethic they had and not impact their children. Through the years, their creativity and resourcefulness got inside my head, inside my bones, became a part of my skin, and etched itself on my heart.

My family's own-your-own business, earn-your-own-money, laziness-is-not-accepted work ethic hit me before I was even a teenager. As a boy I delivered newspapers, I sold Avon products, and I even sold vegetables from my mother's garden. And that work ethic stayed with me as I entered the ministry. I started off with only ten members in my storefront church, so of course not only did I keep my day job, I also worked odd jobs to support my family and the church.

My siblings were equally affected by our parents and their expectations for us. We were taught to be creative, to build our own, to do whatever had to be done. Today, my brother is a Realtor and my sister is an author. We all know how to work with what we've been given; we're all entrepreneurial in some way. And it wasn't just us. In various ways, my cousins and other kin are all entrepreneurs, too.

Hone Your Hustle

Sadly, my father died when he was forty-eight years old and I was only sixteen. The doctors said that his cause of death was renal failure brought on by hypertension, but I disagree. That may be the medical explanation, but I believe my father died due to his inability to transition from struggling to soaring. His business could have done so much better and my father would not have had to work so hard if he had just learned the basics of business. I truly believe that his janitorial operation would have soared if he'd had a bigger vision for its potential and gotten the know-how to manage it properly.

My father's vision was limited, plus he never had the administrative, management, and leadership training necessary to take the tremendous opportunity he'd created with his janitorial service and turn it into a larger success. To this day I can't help but wonder what my father might have been if he'd been able to build a bigger vision for his life, and then, on a practical level, hung up his mops, handed over his brooms and buffers to his employees, and traded those responsibilities for developing a business plan, a marketing strategy, and monthly reports. If my father had been able to catch that vision and make that shift, I am convinced it would have ensured his success. He may have lived a longer life without the constant stress that goes with a hustler's mentality.

While it's important to have a vision and that drive, that hustler's mentality, inside you, that longing to be your own boss and run your own business, it's not enough. As necessary and commendable as that kind of work ethic may be, you still need to make a shift if you want to fly and soar to new heights. Otherwise, you will keep circling and hovering within small, familiar spaces. If you want to soar, then you must hone your hustle into the engine of an entrepreneur.

Fight for Your Flight

When I travel into inner cities where the economy has slowed to a crawl, I see people trying to survive. Some are selling illegal substances, others peddle black market electronics or designer merchandise, others take in cleaning, drive for Uber, haul garbage, help people move, or offer some other service they can provide. They're young and old alike, teens and trailblazers scrambling to keep their heads above water.

But such economic intensity occurs not only in the urban 'hood, because when I travel to Manhattan and walk down Fifth Avenue or Wall Street, I pass well-dressed professional men and women rushing to advise clients and to meet with merchandisers, working late hours, and doing whatever it takes to reach optimum potential. I see vendors selling hot dogs, tacos, and roasted nuts from temporary carts, young street performers playing guitars and singing in the park or near the subway station with an upturned hat for donations.

They're all entrepreneurs in their own way, using what they deem most marketable in exchange for necessities, mortgages, and student loans or just to buy something to eat. Some have a vision that they want to build and may be striving to get ahead and enjoy luxury products and exotic vacations, to save for their retirement, or to purchase a nicer home. Some may even be desperate or misguided in their pursuit, but none are lazy or apathetic about human survival. They all have a reason for doing what they're doing—and that's where you, too, must begin.

If you want to shift from expending energy trying to get off the ground to actually flying as an entrepreneur, then you must identify your motivations. For many of us, economic advancement may seem the obvious goal fueling the internal engine of our ambition, but I must caution you that if making money is your primary motivation for launching a new venture, then you are automatically limiting how high you can fly. Yes, you can build your flying machine and get it off the ground, and you may even be able to remain airborne for a considerable amount of time. At some point, however, you will become so fatigued with jet lag from your journey that you will easily and quickly walk away.

Making a profit is certainly a major indicator of a healthy business, and entrepreneurs want to succeed financially as much as anyone. But they also want to create something, to build a new kind of product or service or invention that is uniquely their own.

21

Others will have gone before them and started similar restaurants, dry cleaning businesses, salons, and fashion boutiques, but none of their predecessors will have utilized the exact same combination of resources filtered through their one-of-a-kind blend of imagination, inspiration, and innovation. For the entrepreneur, making money only creates more opportunities for enhancement, advancement, and expansion.

There's nothing wrong with being motivated by the desire to make more money and elevate your family's lifestyle; however, when money becomes your primary motivator, you will typically stall out rather quickly. If you're only concerned about your profit margins and not the big picture of your business as a whole, you will cut corners for short-term gains and lose sight of qualitative aspects of your endeavor.

In the Bible we're told, "For the love of money is a root of all kinds of evil. Some people, eager for money, have wandered from the faith and pierced themselves with many griefs" (1 Tim. 6:10). Notice it's not money that's the problem—it's our love for it above all else. Financial motivation must be tempered by a clear vision of what you want to accomplish and the sheer passion for whatever field, industry, cause, or product you hope to bring to the rest of the world. You must also have a passion for adventure, for discovery, for new people and places if you want your vision to keep a balanced perspective and to reach new heights.

Broken Wings and Busted Dreams

In addition to complementing the financial motivation to be an entrepreneur, your passion will also help you to take risks, learn from your mistakes, and practice perseverance. If you want a secure, sure-thing, consistent career, then you should probably take a safe job in a field such as accounting, technology, or human resources in a well-established, conservative corporation. While there are no guarantees anymore, you can at least take the safest route possible if you know you are risk averse.

If your personal vision is to have more autonomy, freedom, and flexibility, however, then you may indeed be cut out for being a pilot of possibility in the world's entrepreneurial airspace. Make no mistake, you will probably work harder and longer as an entrepreneur than as someone else's employee. So once again, check your motives and make sure you're not expecting to retire to a tropical island as soon as your business becomes profitable. Entrepreneurs are willing to work harder than ever before as they pursue the fulfillment of something deep within them.

In fact, some unique issues make entrepreneurial flight harder for minorities, the impoverished, and those in underserved communities. None of us gets to choose the giants we must fight, and any obstacles were in place before we ever got here. The turbulence we're suffering at our present altitude may be the result of someone else's past piloting or temporary hijacking. The suffering of those crushed beneath the aftermath of Wall Street bailouts and the resulting debris of layoffs and downsizing left us all struggling to build on the equity of our parents' generations.

It doesn't help that recent political shenanigans leave us in the wake of economic uncertainty as we manage the traumatic despair that erupts when we are uncertain about tomorrow. Even those who have gainful employment do not escape the mounting stress. A whopping 76 percent of Americans live from paycheck to paycheck, according to a recent CNN report. Families who have easier access to capital have often used and abused debt to the degree that their debt-to-income ratio has sunk so low that they now live with daily trepidation wondering if they will be next to walk the plank and be cast into the abyss of homelessness and despair.

This kind of insatiable anxiety can consume anyone. We are many ages, ethnicities, and intellects. We are atheists, agnostics, faith based or fear filled. We are right wing and left wing. The diversity of people who need additional income is amazing. Some are neither left nor right but feel like they have lost their wings altogether. And even if they've flown before, their past crashes have left them with broken wings and busted dreams, wondering if they have missed their only opportunity to reach the height of their God-given potential.

We have a responsibility to help our brothers and sisters navigate through the turbulence and find ways to achieve beyond traditional methods. I can't, in good conscience, ignore the extreme cry for more economic solvency coming from underserved communities in our country. While some people will always be exploitive and opportunistic, most are merely fighting every day for dreams deferred. They are people of faith and clarity, hopes and dreams, desires and decisions, all wondering how or even if they can harvest the unleashed potential waiting to be realized within them.

Some have resorted to petty crime; some are vulnerable to get-rich-quick schemes and the variety of scams that promise a quick win. Some have swallowed their pride and accepted low-income jobs, while others moved back home with their parents. We have college students flipping burgers with dormant degrees and with student loans bigger than the golden arches where they work. Americans come home at night exhausted from the pace around us, the fear inside us. We know we are grounded, out of balance, and operating in the red, trying to survive a deflated existence in an inflated income world.

Then there's Mr. and Mrs. Middle America who in previous times were economically productive and well able to see a brighter future. They, too, have to rethink themselves. They've traded their summer vacations for backyard picnics and gone from the mall to the yard sale for discretionary purchases as they strain within their shrinking budget. Going out to dinner has succumbed to "will work for food" signs of the times.

Undeniably, many of us have created our own chaos. We are reaping the harvest from no vision, poor choices, bad marriages, bankruptcies, poor investments, living beyond our means, the downsizing of a company, and other human maladies. Obstacles ranging from self-induced problems to systemic bias frequently deter the fulfillment of our goals. And regardless of background or ethnicity, I see all of us busier than we've ever been. The pace of life is fast and ferocious. Some of us are so busy trying to survive that we don't get a chance to rethink our goals and recalibrate our practices so as to be more fruitful and effective.

But those who sit back passively waiting on government funding or a start-up investor to knock on their door will be disappointed. Success doesn't trickle down. It springs up from inside a heart that beats to the drum of creativity until its gushing reverberation brings change to the entire community. Are you willing to fight to ignite your flight?

There is no better time than right now to rekindle the embers of long-abandoned dreams or to spark new ones. You can make different choices than the ones that have gotten you where you are now. You can take action and cultivate new habits that will transform your dreams into a business unlike any other, one that uniquely reflects the variety of facets in your extraordinary personality.

One that boldly dares to go where no one has gone before!

A New Model for Momentum

Taking responsibility for your own success must be foundational if you are to succeed as an entrepreneur. I was raised to believe that the goal of young adults is to leave the nest and test their wings—in other words, to go to school and graduate in the hope of landing a lifelong position. Or at least take up a trade and work the next forty or fifty years in the hope of ending up with a gold watch and a bakery cake at their retirement party. However, with 40 percent of our workforce remaining unemployed or underemployed, with a middle class whose shrinking base resembles the man with the withered hand, we need to draw on the creativity that lies in all of us to pull ourselves up as best we can with what we've been given to work with.

We cannot leave ourselves at the mercy of who will or will not hire us. This means that the wings you used to arrive at your present perch may not have the strength, stamina, and span to carry you to where you are going. Trying to soar on wings like eagles is exhausting when all you have left is a handful of feathers! Could it be possible that you've gone as far as you can go with your present wings? Changing times may require a paradigm shift in your vision and a major adjustment to your life's flight plan.

It may be time to chart a new course and engage a new model, to discover new fuel for your creative engines and test new materials, lighter and stronger, to lift you off the ground. What your parents modeled for you was acute wisdom for the era in which they lived. But our day requires untested methods, unexpected mentors, and unconventional models. We cannot fulfill our destiny by simply imitating our parents or repeating our mentor's model. This parakeet style of living where you repeat only what you heard leaves you trapped in a cage of past paradigms, unable to launch yourself into the freedom of exploring limitless skies above you.

If you believe in a power beyond yourself, then you can understand the power of faith to fuel the jet engines of your vision and the new ventures revving up inside you. We were created in the likeness of a creative God so that we can draw on that creativity for the innovation required to reimagine ourselves, reinvent our circumstances, and reinvest our gifts. Getting your vision off the ground and then soaring enables you to move beyond the breach of our times, close the gap between the so-called haves and have-nots, and offer your children a blueprint of passionate pursuit. Your flight pattern will not only assure your ascent, it will also lift your family and raise your community, which should be the inherent goal shared by all of us.

Divine Lift

As you assess your current location and motivation for being an entrepreneur, do not be discouraged by the size or number of obstacles in your path. If you can catch a vision for it then God can do it! There is absolutely no doubt in my mind that God provides the ultimate wind beneath our wings, the divine lift of a curious coincidence or conspicuous conversation. I have seen him open doors beyond my wildest dreams. I know what it is to sit in a seat in life that only a God who loves me immeasurably would provide. I have seen him elevate paupers into philanthropists and cashiers into CEOs, activists into actors and daydreamers into designers.

God is the ultimate strategist and opens doors that no human could have opened. But we must also remember the incredible responsibility and opportunity he reserved for us to create. Consider that God never made a table. He never created a chaise or a chair. He never gave us pencils to write with or paper to write upon. God Almighty never created a box for storage, nor a crate for shipping!

Did he not know that we would need them? Of course the omniscient God of the universe knew what we would need! Yet he never once stooped down to make any of the items we would need every day to survive. Instead, he gave us trees, beautiful, strong, majestic spirals that point ever upward toward heaven. He gave us trees because he knew that trees, if used properly, would provide us with the raw resource to imagine and create specific objects we would need, in the shape we would like, to fit the room we would live in, in the color of our choice!

Are you using all the resources God has placed in your life and dropped in your lap? I suspect most of us do not. Building your vision ever higher is about assessing the time, talents, and treasures we've been given in this lifetime and taking ownership of the choices, the relationships, and the opportunities we have been given. I want to challenge you to see tables in trees, boxes in bushes, and provision in problems!

Often when we are exhausted from dead-end positions, pointless relationships, and indifferent environments, we are forced to change our lives for the good. So don't become weary and faint. If you allow the times to defeat you, the circumstances to deter you, or the obstacles to derail you, it may be because your faith in yourself and even your faith in God has fainted. If any of this remotely sounds like you or someone you love, realize you may be on the precipice of a mighty awakening! It could be possible at this stage in your life, after all you've been through, that you have gathered enough experience from past blunders to set a new course and soar to greater heights!

Many people have succeeded in making this transformation, and I hope that if you have an entrepreneurial inclination you won't allow bad models that you've seen in the past destroy present moments of opportunity. Simply because you have the talent to get somewhere doesn't mean that you have the wisdom to run! You need both the talent and the wisdom, the drive and the directions to reach your destination, and that's why you must make an honest assessment of what drives your desire to be an entrepreneur. You picked up this book for a reason, my friend, and I suspect the timing may be divine.

If you're tired of hovering in place and ready to expand your vision and fly to the next level, then it's time to make your vision a reality.

CHAPTER 2

Winds and Trends

Know Your Conditions

No bird soars in a calm.
—Wilbur Wright

It was the perfect day for making history.

The sky brooded with heavy cloud cover, illuminated by the milky morning light. The chilly temperature, to be expected in the middle of December, hovered in the low 40s, although the 20 mph northerly winds made it feel colder. Propelled by these constant gusts, sand devils danced and dispersed among the many rolling dunes buffering the extended beach.

While these conditions may not sound particularly inviting for a stroll along the seashore, they were indeed perfect for two brothers that day, December 17, 1903, at Kitty Hawk, North Carolina. For you see, those conditions lifted their boxy flying machine off the ground until its engine sustained flight for a full 12 seconds before landing, the first of four successful flights for them that windy day.

Orville and Wilbur Wright knew they had improved their odds for success considerably by choosing such a location. They were not from North Carolina, and in fact had lived in Dayton, Ohio, most of their lives. But as they began tinkering and testing their oversized kites and gliders, mostly built from salvaged parts and what they had on hand at their bicycle shop, the Wright brothers quickly realized their hometown did not have the requisite conditions to get them airborne. They knew they needed a place with steady winds and soft areas for landing, as well as the privacy they desired to work and test their invention uninterrupted.

So they wrote to the National Weather Service and requested data on wind speeds and weather conditions at various sites along the East Coast. After studying the information and averages of potential locations, the Wrights chose a small group of mostly deserted islands, known as the Outer Banks, along the coast of North Carolina. With little to no buffer from weather coming off the Atlantic, these islands endured near constant, often gale-force winds. Mostly comprised of sand dunes and beach grass, the islands also afforded gentle landing strips for the likely abrupt descents the brothers might experience while perfecting their aircraft. And because the weather was so harsh much of the time, the islands had few inhabitants, providing the desired privacy to conduct their work.

If you're like me, you probably haven't thought much about why the Wright brothers chose Kitty Hawk as the site of their history-making milestone. Like many monumental moments from the high points of history, their triumph is one we all learned about in school. But rarely do we consider the years of painstaking work, heartbreaking disappointments, and furious determination that went into that first flight. And even if we know some of the trials the brothers endured before their triumph in the sky, we might not realize just how important locale and weather patterns were to their ultimate success.

The Wright brothers knew if you want to soar, you must study winds and trends.

Check the Weather

As I've already stressed, many people have a vision to become entrepreneurs but are unable to commit to the demands of building a business from scratch. The reality is you can't be committed to the dream and attain it. You have to be committed to the *process* of putting your dream into *practice*. The Wright brothers obviously loved the idea of sailing through the skies with a bird's-eye view of the world, but they had to commit to a long and arduous process to get there.

Like the Wrights and many other entrepreneurial pioneers of our past, when you commit to the process, you are promising to faithfully persevere when confronted by the problems that inevitably impede the launch of any new venture. Committing to the process requires understanding that the greatest education comes from the richest experiences. In fact, success without process will leave you unqualified to reign over what you've built. It is the process that builds your stamina, your insight, and most importantly your relationships, which are the lifeblood of any business.

Once you're committed to the process, then you can begin defining your new venture and creating something that will get you off the ground. But this process begins by studying the economic and social weather patterns all around you, because in order for your business to take flight you must determine the best direction and identify the optimal conditions for launching your dream.

You must recognize, just as the Wright brothers quickly grasped, that the direction of the wind and its weather patterns not only determine if you get off the ground, but once you're airborne, these same meteorological metrics greatly affect how long you remain there. Like the early pioneers of flight, you must learn to read winds and trends and adjust your flight plans accordingly.

Building your new venture and getting it off the ground, you will inevitably experience many of the same metaphoric obstacles the Wright brothers faced and eventually overcame. But you can also learn from many of their strategic decisions. You see, many new businesses fail not because they weren't well designed or didn't have a good business plan but because their owners overlooked the external environment where their products and services would fly. Successful entrepreneurs check the economic, social, and cultural weather before they design their business, let alone try to fly.

In this chapter, I want to share with you some of the winds and trends you must consider even before you design your business and attempt to get it off the ground. Intimately knowing the environment where your business will operate provides you with all kinds of data to help you make decisions about your design, your delivery, and your destination.

You can only ignore these factors at your own risk. Even if you become airborne flying against the wind, you cannot sustain your flight that way indefinitely. Today, more than a hundred years since that first flight, pilots still learn how to work with wind currents and weather patterns in order to fly successfully.

You must do the same.

Which Way the Wind Blows

What happened on the back of a breeze in December of 1903 a few miles from Kitty Hawk, North Carolina, was no accident. Two men dedicated themselves and their resources to doing the groundwork needed to get their flying machine off the ground. They knew where they needed to go to do what had to be done in order to fly. You, too, must investigate the conditions around you in order to determine the best direction for your dream's ascent.

How can you make the winds and trends of your present environment work to give you the lift you need? And where can you land softly while you're tinkering with operations to get the bugs out? Having a contingency plan for changing variables is always a good idea. We will explore such contingencies in more detail in Chapter 5, but it's not too soon to be anticipating what could and might go wrong as you ramp up for takeoff. Whether you end up succeeding with your plan A or with plan Z, all your plans require paying close attention to specific details within your environment as well as identifying ongoing patterns.

Sometimes this means working from the *inside out*—knowing your ultimate goal and working backward from it. The Wright brothers knew they wanted to invent a sustainable, controllable flying machine, and as they worked through their process they identified the atmospheric elements required for the optimal opportunity to succeed. Then they researched their options and chose Kitty Hawk. Many times you know what you want to offer, sell, or provide but you haven't considered what your business needs to flourish.

When I recently decided to dip my toes into the waters of daytime television with my own show, I approached it from the inside out. While I had experience with television, production, and generating inspiring content, I also knew there was still so much I didn't know. My production partner, Tegna Media, excelled as a bundler of syndicated programming but had not created original content—my show would be a new venture for them as well.

We both had experience in the airspace where we wanted to fly, but neither of us had built and flown the kind of plane necessary to soar there. In order to gauge the weather in the daytime talk show atmosphere, I could think of no better forecaster than Oprah, who was happy to share her wisdom with me. As my friend, she encouraged me, but as a professional she also cautioned me about stormy weather at the altitude to which my show aspired.

"The winds have changed," she explained, "since I started my show back in the day." She went on to explain that when she first launched her daytime program, only three major networks controlled the majority of programming. Cable channels and independent programming were just starting to gain the momentum that would usher in a huge shift in viewing options and opportunities. The Internet and online viewing had not exploded into our cultural consciousness with the myriad of selections we have today. As a result of changing technology, most of the latest estimates reveal that traditional television channels have lost 30 to 40 percent of their viewership to streaming services from independent media providers such as Netflix, Hulu, and Amazon.

Oprah's style of talk show was also something fresh and groundbreaking for its time. The competition she faced was mostly focused on the extremes of old-fashioned celebrity interviews or the new sensational tabloid-style shows bringing melodramatic outbursts to the small screen. While at first she flirted with both ends of this spectrum, she quickly realized she wanted to provide substance, inspiration, and encouragement to her viewers in ways they weren't getting them anywhere else. Even though I aspired to similar goals with my show, I knew the potential audience was already aware of this style of talk show.

With this knowledge of climate change, I knew before I ever started that I would be flying against the wind. It wasn't that I couldn't succeed or wouldn't reach my destination; it was simply going to require more effort and take longer to get there. For this reason, some sponsors and syndication clients chose not to purchase and broadcast my show. It wasn't that they disliked me or the kind of program I offered. It wasn't that they didn't want me to succeed. It was simply their awareness of how this show would be flying against the wind.

It's the same phenomenon you experience when flying against or with the jet stream. When I fly from my home in Dallas to Los Angeles, it usually takes around three hours. Flying west, my plane has to fight against a strong headwind that provides powerful resistance, forcing the plane's engines to work harder and go slower to cover the same distance. On the return trip, however, it's only about two hours or less because of the strong tailwind.

The winds had changed and were more erratic than ever for the kind of show I wanted to do. Because this was a new venture for Tegna and me, and because we knew we were going against the wind, we made sure we hired only the very best producers, set designers, tech operators, stylists, and support staff. We deliberately sought out experts with experience in daytime talk shows, people who could help us navigate the turbulence we were anticipating. These other team members were my Kitty Hawk, helping me have what I needed to get my show off the ground and providing soft spots to land when I made a mistake.

After completing one season, I decided the airspace was too crowded and the turbulence too great for me to continue. It wasn't that I didn't want to keep working harder than ever before or hated commuting between Dallas and Los Angeles, and it wasn't that I didn't believe we could gain viewership and improve the program. It was simply a matter of what Oprah told me: the winds had changed.

And because I have many other ventures that consume my energy and attention, I didn't have the patience and drive to devote myself singularly to navigating that airspace. So I decided to take what I had learned and land the plane while the choice was still my own!

Your Slice of the Pie

The other way to explore your environment for clues on how to design your business plan is to look at what needs fixing, changing, or solving. This method looks from the *outside in* and isolates a problem or condition currently affecting the social and cultural climate around us. You may notice the need for a new product or invention to help people handle lifestyle changes due to technology, the economy, or migration patterns. You may see an opportunity that appeals to certain demographics or regional interests.

Similarly, you may see the spark of a new trend and fan it into a full-blown wildfire. This means seeing something good and knowing it can be made better, perhaps through exposure and promotion to a wider audience. It's the reason we see so many copycat products and businesses follow in the wake of a major success. If a certain genre of TV show or movie explodes, then you can be certain that similar ones will follow.

Sometimes the weather changes to your advantage without any attempt to influence it yourself. You may not even know what caused the wind to shift until after the storm has hit. For instance, this kind of phenomenon recently occurred with the mega-talented Patti LaBelle. Known as the Godmother of Soul, she had enjoyed a decades-long career as a singer, performer, and actress. Not content to rest on her lyrical laurels, Patti drew on her culinary talents and closed a deal with Walmart to sell her delicious sweet potato pies. Like the talented entrepreneur she is, Patti used her brand identity to expand from making music to making dessert.

While the pies sold well, they didn't explode until a superfan named James Wright posted a three-minute video on YouTube in which he hilariously tasted the pie and sang its praises like

Patti—literally. Almost overnight, his post received more than five million hits and sent sales of Patti's pies into the stratosphere. Suddenly, Walmart couldn't keep them in stock and people were selling them for ten times the retail price on eBay! Patti said she knew something was up when she noticed she was selling more pies than records.

The best marketing genius probably could not have come up with a promotional pitch as funny and authentic as James Wright's. But nonetheless, his online taste test changed the weather patterns around Patti's pies. Not only did she increase production to meet customers' demands, she launched an entire line of goodies called Patti's Good Life, including other pies, cobblers, and sweets. Wright's viral sensation changed the weather, and she changed to meet its new opportunities.

One Size Never Fits All

Many would-be entrepreneurs tell me they aren't "creative" enough to come up with an original idea, invention, or innovation. And I always say, "No problem—just take something people want or need in your area and do it better than anyone else!" Scripture tells us that "there is nothing new under the sun" (Ecc. 1:9), and I suspect this holds true for small businesses as much as for anything else. The basics that all humans need—food and drink, shelter, clothing—continue to sustain millions of businesses in the form of restaurants, hotels, and boutiques, just to name a few.

Just consider how many coffee shops there are near your home or office. You probably have more than one Starbucks within a five-mile radius, along with at least one other nationally franchised brewery such as Caribou Coffee, Gloria Jean's, Death Wish, Costa, Biggby, and It's a Grind. Then there are likely at least one or two independent shops, the kind where you might have met the owner, the kind where the pace is a little slower, the muffins a little fresher, the service a little better, and the atmosphere a little cozier.

I'm able to describe these little extras not because I've been spying in your neighborhood but because I know that in order to compete with the big chains, any locally owned business, particularly in the food and beverage service, must offer something extra—extra care, extra attention, extra service, extra quality—so as to compete for your regular business.

So think about something you either want or need regularly. Maybe it involves solving a problem you yourself face on a regular basis. For instance, do you lack the time to do laundry and ironing and wish there was a service that took extra care in making your professional wardrobe look like new? One that delivered to your home and made the process as simple and dependable as possible? One that recognizes and respects the differences in caring for linen versus Lycra?

Sure, there may be three other laundry services in town, but they serve corporate customers more than individuals. The issue, as we will see in a moment, then becomes the number of other customers like yourself within your area—as well as your new venture's location and the overall economic outlook of your city. But the process often starts with identifying a business you yourself would frequent.

Surprisingly enough, one of the small businesses that's recently started making a comeback is the local independent bookstore. From young millennials to older boomers, customers are realizing how much they enjoy having a family-friendly community gathering place that sells books, fosters relationships through reading clubs and study groups, and provides a relaxing atmosphere where people can enjoy a latte or glass of wine. Savvy bookstore owners are realizing their target customers may not be professionals seeking the latest business book as much as they're simply younger parents looking for an alternative to the library.

Timing Is Everything

You can take any product, service, or consumer solution and improve upon it. And the best improvements customize it to your location and customer base and the overall context. Opening a high-end dress boutique for young professional women in an urban area where factories have closed and residents are mostly retirees who can't afford to move obviously does not make good business sense. On the other hand, if you've noticed abandoned factories being converted into lofts downtown right next to new clubs and restaurants, then your boutique could be right on the cusp of a new wave of urban gentrification.

But you must do your homework and interpret the data with common sense, objective clarity, and personal instinct. When I got ready to buy my house, I wanted to check its value against others in the neighborhood, and I also wanted to determine the direction the city was growing. Was my investment in this house likely to retain its value, or better yet, yield an increase? Or was growth moving in a direction likely to cause this property to decrease in value?

Many cities seem to go back and forth, oscillating between a thriving downtown with minimal suburban residents and a city that has sprawled into its suburbs, leaving the downtown an empty shell. Dallas was built up in the 1970s, during the oil and gas boom, around a dichotomy between work and home. At the time, bread-winners would work downtown but didn't want to live there, instead taking their families to the suburbs to live in a nice house with a two-car garage and a swing set in the backyard. That trend has now reversed at least a couple of times, and now condos and town houses have replaced the split-level ranch homes of a bygone era.

Timing is crucial when you're trying to catch winds strong enough to get your plane off the ground. No matter how good your product or service, if there's no wind behind it, you won't succeed. What works for one season won't work for another. I recall how years ago when my book *Woman, Thou Art Loosed!* was exploding, we had an opportunity to partner with Thomas Nelson to produce a special edition *Woman, Thou Art Loosed!* Bible. In addition to my notes, commentary, and questions, this Bible was packaged in the shape of a woman's pocketbook in an attempt to make it unique, stylish, portable, and easy to carry. Response was tremendous and many people told me they were blessed by it.

Nonetheless, I'm keenly aware that the book might not have succeeded if launched in today's cultural and economic climate. Ebooks have replaced hard copies, and now the YouVersion Bible app, a free version of the NIV Bible, receives more downloads than any other version sells. Also, with the popularity of designer purses by Coach, Louis Vuitton, and others, I'm not sure our unique design would be as appealing to women now as it was then.

We frequently see the way timing affects both popularity and the price point of products, particularly with technology. I recall reading that when Apple was first launching its unique computers, sales were sluggish, largely because the technology was still new and the price point was very high. As more and more people began using computers, new companies sprang up to meet demand, which increased competition and lowered prices. Over time, conditions changed and Apple computers became more affordable and established themselves as a unique brand.

As Malcolm Gladwell explains so brilliantly in *The Tipping Point*, there's a pivotal juncture where a business goes from seeking new customers to having new customers seek it. You want to do all you can to design your business to survive until you reach that point and then to thrive once you're on the other side of it. Yet one more reason to pay close attention to the entrepreneurial climate and economic weather of your environment. While you may not be able to control the clock with regard to all aspects of your product, you must still know what time it is!

Sizing Up Your Situation

Whether you're responding to winds and trends from the inside out or outside in, both require you to be a problem-solver. No matter how much passion, hard work, and dedication you pour into your venture, if it doesn't solve an identifiable problem for customers willing to pay for your solution, it will never get off the ground. Or if it does, then it will likely arc across the sky like fireworks instead of like an F-16. So I advise you to begin by recruiting a problem that a significant number of people would be willing to pay you to solve for them.

Even before you begin taking stock of your resources and building your business, the most important thing you as an entrepreneur must have is a problem to fix. Until your business is an answer, you will not be successful. Building a business because you want money will generally lead to failure. Building a business for the ego boost of saying, "I own my own business!" may make great conversation at social events. But if you want to build an equitable business, it isn't capital that you need more than anything else to get started on the right foot—it's a juicy problem. Once you find your problem, you will find an investor motivated to help you fix it.

The best kinds of entrepreneurial problems often revolve around something lacking within a specific region that could sustain a business. Whether it's the lack of a dry cleaner in an area where many professional people have just moved or the need for a beauty salon within a diverse, predominantly female community, the need can be isolated and quantified.

On the other hand, you may have an extraordinary product or service that you believe transcends geographical or demographic limits. You know you want to launch this endeavor online to maximize your exposure and build the largest customer base possible. Nonetheless, you must still complete your due diligence and come up with the best strategy for reaching the customers or clients who need what you've got. While it's true the Internet has opened vast territories of connectivity that facilitate incredible opportunities for commerce, you will still need to make a plan.

Whether you begin with a problem involving something lacking or something offered, your process must include market research to identify the area you anticipate serving, the size and demographics of your customer base, and your competition. Each is a vital piece of the puzzle that will become your flight plan and the blueprint for your business. Let's briefly consider them.

Your Area of Service

What are the physical parameters of the area you want to service with your products? I encourage you to get a map and outline your territory in a bold color that's easily seen. If you're offering an online product or service and you truly hope to appeal to a global consumer base, I would still try to identify the countries, regions, and cities where your odds for success are greatest.

You must also keep in mind that all distances are not equal within the business world. Focusing on a five-block radius of service might keep your pizza parlor thriving in New York or Chicago, but you will more likely need to consider a five- or ten-mile area in smaller cities and suburban areas. Depending on your specific product offering, you must remember that distance is relative and must be measured through the eyes of your customers. Which brings us to...

Your Customer Base—Size and Demographics

No matter how large and broad you want your customer base to be, the reality is that most entrepreneurial efforts tend to attract one core group. "But, Bishop Jakes," you say, "I'm wanting to sell my delicious pound cakes online. Everyone loves pound cake, right? So I need to target as many people as possible!"

While I appreciate the optimism of such logic, this thinking makes a crucial, erroneous assumption. Just because most people (not everyone—not the dieters, not the people allergic to gluten, not the people who simply prefer pie over cake!) seem to love your delicious pound cake doesn't mean that everyone will find you online. And of those who do find you, not all of them will have the means or be inclined to order a pound cake they haven't tasted yet.

In order to find the potential customers who do love pound cake and are looking to order one online, you must do further research and try to learn as much as possible about the current online baked-goods industry. Is pound cake really viable when everyone else seems to be succeeding with cupcakes? Are you prepared for large, corporate orders? What if American Express wants to order a thousand of your pound cakes to send to their best customers? Will you offer more than one flavor of cake? Will you allow customers to make special requests?

On and on the questions go, and as soon as you answer one question, two more pop up in its place. Sometimes you can narrow your scope and target a more select customer base by learning as much as possible about the core group of consumers you want to target.

These may be the people most likely to purchase your product or the ones you believe would benefit from your product the most.

Let's say, for example, you want to start small with your online cake business and appeal to families looking for sweets "like Momma used to bake" for special occasions—birthdays, anniversaries, family reunions, Thanksgiving, Christmas, and other holidays. You've eliminated corporate clients with large orders for the time being and instead want to connect with people too busy to cook who still want something delicious and home baked.

Such people are also going to want the cake to be affordable, because if your price is too much more than it costs them to bake it themselves or buy elsewhere, you will lose them. We'll discuss production costs and pricing strategies in Chapter 5, but you still have to keep in mind what your customers will be willing to pay. You have to know how they perceive the value of what you're offering.

Now that you've narrowed your target customer base, you would be wise to find out as much about the customer as possible: average age, marital status and average size of household, whether they rent or own their home, their ethnicity, average income, level of education, and number of hours typically spent working each week.

While these large indicators may be obvious to you, I encourage you to also consider trying to determine where your targeted customers tend to shop most—online or in a bricks-and-mortar store. How much do they usually spend on food each week? How often do they eat dessert or purchase sweets? Do their habits change for special occasions? What are the other brands they are likely to purchase? Which brings us to...

Your Competition

One of the most valuable assets you have for determining which way your wind is blowing comes from studying your competition. Learn as much about them as you possibly can. And don't overlook experiencing your competition as a customer would, making note of all the details from the first contact until you conclude your transaction. How can you improve the way you interact with your customers? How can you train future employees accordingly?

Businesses that have failed while attempting to provide your product or service often prove as valuable as success stories in helping you learn what does and doesn't work. If you can identify and talk with some of these other entrepreneurs, then all the better. Don't assume that they will automatically refuse to discuss the business with you. You would be surprised how much they're willing to share. Flat-out ask them to tell you what they wished they had known before they started their venture. There may be numerous ways you can help each other, increasing the profitability of both businesses.

Divine Design

When I first became a pastor back in West Virginia, I didn't need a flying machine to minister to my flock. I preached God's Word, helped those in need, buried the dead, and married the wed! It was all spiritual work and fit within the gravitational pull of the pulpit. As our church grew and opportunities increased, I realized I couldn't keep doing things the way I'd been doing them. When I talk with young pastors today, most of them tell me they assumed they were starting a church that needed to function like a successful business. But back in my early days, I had to fly by the seat of my pants until I could build a plane big enough to carry my dreams.

With so many possible ways to affect our nation and the world, to minister through radio and TV and online technology, I felt very much like the Wright brothers must have felt. I needed to build something to get me from point A to point B. I had to add staff members, expand facilities, employ experts in technology, along with developing the various support systems needed to sustain them all.

Now, more than three hundred employees later, I have built a flying machine that serves both my ministry and my entrepreneurial endeavors. The employees' skills include graphic design, shipping and receiving, catering, music and film production, and a variety of other areas I never imagined needing to support my work. But in order to grow, in order to fulfill the potential that God gave me and make the most of the opportunities He presented, I had to be willing to invent something all my own, a divine-inspired design.

You, too, must look at the distance between where you are and where you want to go. Then you can begin building your own machine to take you there. You won't be able to do it all by yourself, but by the same token, it all starts with you putting your dream in motion. You can't fly it, maintain it, and take it higher if you weren't involved in its original construction!

Your machine must weather all kinds of conditions, some you know about already and others you can only discover once you're in the air. That's why you must keep your finger raised to gauge the force and direction of the winds around you. That's why you must be prepared for changes in the temperature and weather patterns of your cultural climate. Winds and trends can cause something as formidable and seemingly indestructible as the *Titanic* to sink. But they can also be harnessed to empower your ability to take flight and soar!

CHAPTER 3

Damsel, Arise!

When the Wind Is Blowing Your Way

And when he was come in, he saith unto them, Why make ye this ado, and weep? the damsel is not dead, but sleepeth. And they laughed him to scorn. But when he had put them all out, he taketh the father and the mother of the damsel, and them that were with him, and entereth in where the damsel was lying. And he took the damsel by the hand, and said unto her, *Talitha cumi*; which is, being interpreted, Damsel, I say unto thee, arise.

—Mark 5:39–42 KJV

Has the 609 come in yet?" my mother asked. "What about 607?" We were sitting outside on the patio of my home in Texas, enjoying the mild spring weather and watching my dogs frolic in our backyard. Although my mother had been diagnosed with Alzheimer's at the time she asked these questions, they made perfect sense to me.

"Yes, ma'am," I said. "I believe all the properties are up to date."

"That's good," she said, smiling to herself. "What a blessing they have been."

I agreed with her, knowing that her observation was a huge understatement. You see, up until the time she passed away, my mother owned seven rental properties back in West Virginia where we lived when I was growing up. She had always identified each one and called it by the house number of its street address.

Now, my mother had owned these properties for years. She had the foresight when she was a younger woman to invest her resources in anticipation of a day when her income would be fixed or limited, and her wisdom clearly paid off. Despite the devastating debilitation of the disease that dulled her razor-sharp mind, my mother still remembered each property and its specifics much better than I could.

My mother was forward thinking and determined to take her well-being and the future of her family into her own hands. She had always been a progressive thinker and was never limited to one stream of income. In addition to teaching school, she would sell Avon from our home, raise vegetables that I would peddle door to door, and do anything else she could to help my dad support our family. From the meager income she and my father generated from their tireless endeavors, my mother managed to put away a little money until she had a nest egg ready to hatch for the purchase of her first rental property. Once she purchased this little house up the street from our home, she began saving again until she had enough to buy another. Eventually she had several houses through which she had padded her future.

I'll never forget being a boy and sitting in our living room one afternoon as she met with a married couple from a neighborhood several miles from where she had first bought property. They owned a little cottage for sale down the street from where they lived. They had agreed to close the deal and sign the papers for my mother's purchase that day. The three of them had negotiated terms already, and the owners had agreed to carry the loan my mother needed for the purchase. While the husband was on board with this arrangement, his wife, who didn't really want to sell the property, had a major attitude. After expressing her reluctance to sell yet again, she muttered, "That's all right... we'll get that place back like we always do."

The tension was palpable, but no one said anything as her husband signed the papers and handed the pen to my mother. Maintaining her poker face, Mama signed her name with a flourish, looked up and smiled, and said, "Yeah, when hell freezes over!" I didn't crack a smile then, but I wanted to! After they left, my mother looked at me as we both burst out laughing. She said, "They will *never* get that house back!" She was right, too! That couple died several years later, and true to her word, my mother owned that property for the rest of her life, having quickly paid it off free and clear to establish it as a steady stream of income for decades to come.

Although my mother drew a retirement pension from the Kanawha County Board of Education from her years as a teacher, a career she had before becoming the Equal Employment officer for the state of West Virginia, she had created various income streams for her retirement along with her monthly Social Security check. Mother had made strategic decisions much earlier in her life that were game changers, alleviating the normal pressure associated with fixed-income and retirement plans for most people her age. She had not wanted to count on a bank or the government to control her future earnings and standard of living so she made decisions in 1964 that continued to provide for her in the thirty-five years that followed.

The young working wife and mother she was then made sacrifices and took calculated risks in order to provide for the old woman she would someday become. Following her example, I've done some investing at various times throughout my adult life, buying and selling real estate. What was initially just a mother and son laughing together became a sense of the importance of taking control of my financial future.

My mother modeled a method that gave me the inclination to think for myself and to take the wheel of my destiny and drive in the direction of my dreams. As I reflect on it now, my mother was doing all of this at a time when most people thought a woman's place was in the kitchen! She was an entrepreneur who discovered she could soar.

My mother understood that if you're going to be an effective entrepreneur, in fact if you're going to be a good steward of today, you must know now how to prepare for the future. Those who do are far more likely to thrive while others are left to survive!

Woman, Hear You Roar

I'm not the only entrepreneur inspired by the example of my parents. For many generations, fathers and mothers have passed on habits to help their children unlock their power and creativity by employing more than one method of reliance. Growing up, many of us who were raised in underserved communities watched as our mother and father juggled two, three, even four jobs, doing whatever it took to put food on the table and keep a roof over our heads. Some of them pursued their dreams even while keeping their day job to pay the bills.

Singer-songwriter Valerie June describes the impact of watching her father run two small businesses, one a music production and promotion company and the other a construction and demolition business, on her own career:

> Looking back, I see that my father's companies were his form of art, and I find myself still learning lessons from

the years we worked side by side. Music promotion was his passion, but construction was his source of financial stability. So many times on the path toward manifesting my own musical dream, I have leaned on the work foundation he and my mother laid for us. The things we are passionate about are fueled by mundane tasks. All is necessary. ("The First Time I…Lost a Parent," *New York Times*, p. 6, March 12, 2017)

For many of us, our ability to fly emerged not only from the wings our parents gave us but also from the social season and cultural climate. When I was growing up in the 1960s and '70s, women continued to gain ground in the workplace. In addition to absorbing the example my mother set, growing up I witnessed many women in our community who juggled multiple entrepreneurial endeavors with similar dexterity. In fact, the accountant my parents used for their tax returns and for my mother's real estate deals was Mrs. Theodora Rutherford, a smart black woman who ran her own small business from her home office in Institute, West Virginia.

This was the era when the feminist movement was emerging. Women had burned their bras and ignited their business savvy. They started driving, went back to school, and left the first high-heeled footprints on a glass ceiling that would shatter from the force of tenacious women moving from cookbooks to textbooks. These women became the trend-setting matriarchs prying the lid off the entombment of females in our society and burying male chauvinism in its place!

Women had entered the workforce out of necessity during World War II, and many continued to work afterward as they discovered new abilities and latent talents. Neither the world nor the family would ever be quite the same again. We would spend the next fifty years or more redefining what it meant to be a woman, a mother, and a sister. What was thought to be a temporary trend eventually morphed into a lifestyle.

While television programs kept Aunt Bee cooking in the kitchen and Carol Brady cruising in the car pool, their real-life counterparts were stepping beyond the domestic boundaries of their domiciles into offices, factories, retail shops, and boardrooms. *Feminism* was becoming a word heard with more frequency as pioneers like Gloria Steinem, Barbara Walters, and Shirley Chisholm, the first black woman elected to the United States Congress, paved the way.

Women like these trailblazers not only shattered glass ceilings but also became role models for the generations that followed. They made inroads into virtually every sector of industry and entertainment, inspiring countless little girls to look beyond their Barbie dolls and glimpse themselves as astronauts, accountants, actresses, architects—and, of course, entrepreneurs. No wonder then that the number of female-owned businesses grew by 74 percent from 1997 to 2015, a rate one and a half times the national average of growth, according to a study commissioned and published by American Express OPEN ("2015 State of Women-Owned Businesses Report," http://www.womenable.com/content/userfiles/Amex_OPEN_State _of_WOBs_2015_Executive_Report_finalsm.pdf).

Women now own 30 percent of all businesses in the United States, accounting for more than nine million firms. The study concluded, "The only bright spot in recent years with respect to privately held company job growth has been among women-owned firms." Supporting this conclusion, women-owned businesses have added an estimated 340,000 jobs to the economy since 2007, while employment at companies owned by men (or with equally shared ownership) has declined.

And African American women control 14 percent of these companies, or roughly 1.3 million businesses, which is more than the number of businesses owned by *all* minority women in 1997, according to this same American Express report. In fact, the number of businesses owned by African American women had grown 332 percent since 1997, making black females the fastest growing group of entrepreneurs in the United States. This fact does not surprise me in the least since I grew up watching my mother create something from nothing by honing her natural intelligence and common-sense business acumen.

Never Too Late

Black women spanning a range of ages and stages are the fastest-growing group of entrepreneurs in our country right now. This thriving group of new risk-takers is comprised not only of young women with a recent college degree in their hands. Nor is it mostly composed of young professionals determined to launch a start-up with a group of their friends. Women of every age are discovering their place and entering the spectrum of entrepreneurial opportunities in the global community of our online world.

People no longer stay with one company in one function for the duration of their professional careers. They can operate within a variety of roles in any given industry or even switch career fields altogether in search of the area where they are able to contribute most passionately. Retirement is no longer an option for others who nonetheless long for a change that will awaken their soul and challenge them in new and unexpected ways. It's not uncommon to see individuals embarking on their second, third, or fourth acts as they rewrite the narrative of their own success.

One prime-time example is Robbie Montgomery, a native Mississippian who grew up singing in the church choir and learning how to cook from her mother. Being the oldest of nine children, Robbie had to help prepare meals, and in the process she memorized the recipes for the delicious home cooking for which her mama was known. Little did she know that this culinary talent would later resurface when Robbie left home to pursue a professional singing career. Her vocal talent led her to tour as a backup singer for Ike and Tina Turner, and she later did session work with Dr. John, Joe Cocker, Stevie Wonder, and Barbra Streisand.

When a lung condition did not heal properly, Robbie was forced to end her professional music career, which led her to explore her options. She first explored the field of medicine by working as a dialysis technician. But fortunately for anyone who has ever tasted her short ribs or peach cobbler, Robbie's love of food soon pulled her back to the kitchen and cooking the mouthwatering soul food she had learned to prepare while growing up.

Her story would be a triumphant success if it ended right there, but Miss Robbie's path intersected with that of another Mississippi girl named Oprah Winfrey. Oprah not only loved Miss Robbie's cooking but also partnered with her to create a reality television program for the Oprah Winfrey Network (OWN). *Sweetie Pie's* documents the ups and downs, struggles and successes of running a family business as Miss Robbie and her son Tim Norman try to expand their brand and extend their locations.

Recently while I was in Los Angeles shooting my show, I noticed Sweetie Pie's had just opened a new restaurant in Beverly Hills. A fan of Miss Robbie's as well as of her cooking, I had just enough time in between leaving the set and catching my flight to stop in. The food was as delicious as ever and made me remember the meals my mother and aunts would cook up for Sunday dinners and family gatherings. I took a pic and immediately posted it on Instagram, happy to fulfill the responsibility we have to help each other survive.

Driving away, I reflected that many people know Miss Robbie's food but don't find the lesson in her story. She not only landed on her feet after being forced to switch careers, she also demonstrates the power of leveraging opportunities. It's one thing to be a patron of a business but another thing to market that business as an ambassador of affirmation.

Robbie Montgomery realized her dream to be a professional singer but watched it disappear when her health deteriorated. Instead of lamenting her loss or dwelling on disappointment, she took a risk to transform something she loved into something others would love as well. She turned her talent into a restaurant and catapulted her restaurant into a reality show that gives her extraordinary exposure and enables her to open multiple locations. Learning the power of resilience and perseverance, she refused to settle for a life of regret. She reimagined herself and reinvented her purpose to create food instead of music.

Start Small, Finish Big

Miss Robbie illustrates what I consider to be a core principle for entrepreneurs: start small in order to finish big. Now, please notice I didn't say to dream small—on the contrary, I encourage you to cast big dreams that will stretch your imagination and require you to rely on divine inspiration to sustain you. But you must start where you are and use what you have.

When our dreams exceed our resources and our vision transcends our present opportunities, we must remember to start small even as we strive toward success.

Because start-ups often have few resources to underwrite the early years, many entrepreneurs will have to employ a measured approach to their dreams. It isn't a lack of faith that makes you start small. It is simply the access to capital and the understanding that you may not have the time or necessary resources to devote your full attention to your dream without bankrupting your other responsibilities.

Wisdom necessitates that you consider how much of both time and money you can invest in your dream as you carefully contemplate what is realistically available to you. In short, you cannot play with cards you haven't been dealt. My mother had saved a little money, but with small children and a steady stream of monthly expenses, she needed an investment that didn't consume her time when she was already working.

You have to start where you are. Modify your strategy to fit your realities. But whatever you do, don't remain dormant. You must use what is in your hand! This principle reminds me of the way God instructed Moses when the people of Israel were enslaved in Egypt. God called Moses to confront Pharaoh and to lead his people to the Promised Land, which was a staggering endeavor, but when Moses began making excuses, God told him to start with what he had in his hand.

> Moses answered, "What if they do not believe me or listen to me and say, 'The LORD did not appear to you'?"
>
> Then the LORD said to him, "What is that in your hand?"
>
> "A staff," he replied.
>
> The LORD said, "Throw it on the ground."
>
> Moses threw it on the ground and it became a snake, and he ran from it. Then the LORD said to him, "Reach out your hand and take it by the tail." So Moses reached out and took hold of the snake and it turned back into a staff in his hand. (Exodus 4:1–4)

Moses was no stranger to reinventing himself—and in his case it had been a downward spiral. Rescued by Pharaoh's daughter from a reed basket in the Nile River, Moses was raised as Egyptian royalty, not as a Hebrew slave. Then his temper got the best of him and he killed an Egyptian, forcing Moses to flee into the desert as a fugitive. Perhaps he would have been content to tend sheep and scrape by in the harsh, arid conditions—we don't know. But what we do know is that Moses wasted no time unfolding a grocery list of canned excuses and fresh fears.

God, however, is not interested in Moses' excuses—just as he's not fooled by yours or mine. Instead he simply asks Moses, "What's that in your hand? Let's start with what you've got!" Moses has a huge task in front of him, but he doesn't need to wait until the majority accepts him or he has a huge army or he's a better and less fearful speaker. God basically told Moses to stop waiting and start walking! If you let it, your hesitation will only become a limitation. But starting too big and aiming too high can be just as confining and ultimately destructive.

An old Chinese proverb reminds us that a journey of a thousand miles starts with one step. I would say that a million-dollar empire starts with the one thing you already do well, the one talent, ability, skill, or service that others need. Yes, it would be wonderful to begin with hundreds of thousands of dollars in capital from friendly, patient investors. Yes, it would be fantastic to have a team of talented, hardworking, like-minded colleagues who want to share in the journey to realize your dream.

But every journey, no matter how big, starts with one foot in front of the other. The sky may be your limit, but reality is always your runway. If you want to soar, you first have to flap your wings!

Wanting Patience—and Wanting It Now!

No matter your age or stage of life, you can remain fruitful if you're willing to look inside at what you have in your hand. But starting small and growing your business requires extreme patience, something that's challenging for all of us but that's essential for successful business owners. Such patience is easier for some people—and some generations—than others.

My natural children as well as spiritual ones are largely millennials, born between the early 1980s and early 2000s. I absolutely love their passion but have consistently had to fight their impatience. I am a baby boomer, a builder by nature, born in a time when our nation was growing in every field and frontier. But building anything worth having...takes...time. Struggle is to be expected. So many of my younger mentees starting new ventures, from online apps to record labels to nonprofits, underestimate the ramp-up time required for takeoff. Because they grew up watching their heroes in midflight, they've rarely seen the mistakes, the missteps, and the misunderstandings that are naturally part of any ascent.

Millennials have seen people explode overnight with viral sensations on YouTube channels and ferociously successful friends on Facebook. They're accustomed to the Kardashian brand of success in which anyone can follow their dreams and explode into notoriety for it. Yes, there will be those supernovas, and thanks to social media we will know about them in constant updates of their celebrity status, but they are exceptions not exemplars. *Success is a process that takes time.*

With such shooting stars as their models, many millennials underestimate the ramp-up time required. When their venture doesn't take off and go straight up like a helicopter, they tend to feel like they've failed and want to quit. Delayed doesn't equate to denied! You must have a long-term financial strategy that can sustain your business's steady growth without eating up profits and funds needed for maintenance and expansion. Many people, not just millennials, collapse in their first year because they don't have enough capital to sustain themselves and to invest in the business at the same time.

You may need to start on a part-time basis before launching your venture and seeing if you can afford to hire yourself full-time. My main concern with the helicopter model is that you miss out on pacing yourself and sustaining the hard work that could have ensured your success over time. For example, if you have loans, be sure to count the cost for operating your business but also be reasonable about the time required to become profitable.

I don't want to imply that impatience only attacks the young because it can strike anyone at any age. But I'm convinced that what we had modeled in front of us growing up usually has a direct influence on our expectations and willingness to delay gratification. And expectations are paramount. If you don't expect a process and you run into one, then you will think you're failing when it's just the current stage of the game. Remember, graduation relies on that which is gradual!

Swimming with the Sharks

I love watching the TV show *Shark Tank*, where budding entrepreneurs pitch their product, service, or idea to a seasoned panel of experienced investors, mostly successful CEOs. These would-be investors almost always ask participants how many other investors they have and what those investors have earned so far. Not only do the veteran entrepreneurs want to know with whom they will potentially share profits, they only want to invest in something that has maximized its current level. Otherwise, they know it's going to crash.

Fortunately, you do not have to have wealthy investors or liberal bankers to launch your venture. I suspect now more than ever we have great opportunities to start new businesses with smaller resources than previous dreamers. Harnessing online tools and social media, you can minimize costs while reaching an enormous pool of consumers. I know so many people who have started out small, listed their products on eBay or Etsy or other sites, created a PayPal account, and gained steady momentum. Such opportunities have leveled the playing field for smaller businesses to be born.

Many times, in the early, embryonic stages of launching a new venture, you're so busy doing the business that you don't have time to promote the business. But no matter how great your product, how helpful your service, or how impactful your nonprofit, without promotional awareness targeted at your core constituents, you will founder and ultimately fail. The Bible says, "Neither do men light a candle, and put it under a bushel, but on a candlestick; and it giveth light unto all that are in the house" (Matt. 5:15 KJV).

Having a talent, a skill, a service is not enough. You must be able to manage the business and its growth as well as market it effectively in each stage of development. But promoting and marketing your business may be easier and more cost-effective than ever before. With a few taps on your smartphone, you can send tweets, blogs, banners, and blasts at minimal cost.

If you are in a business where you do something with your own hands—hair care, baking, cosmetology, dentistry, chiropractic—so much energy is involved in doing that there's little time or energy left for planning. But to pick up speed, you must get your hands free! You must have capacity to train others in order to grow and bring in others to your team. Without taking time to step away from your business for a view at 30,000 feet, you will constantly be flying low to the ground.

Being an entrepreneur is a mind-set, not a money set. So if you're wanting to launch your business in the hopes of overnight riches, think again. You must passionately love some aspect of your venture or, like any relationship, the infatuation will quickly fade as practical matters remove the romantic veneer. You must be willing to see the big picture even as you connect the daily dots and focus on the details. You must enjoy being a problem-solver, not just a moneymaker.

The Wind at Your Back

Finally, I encourage you to know the weather patterns of your business's geography. By this I mean make sure you do all the due diligence that can possibly be done to ensure your product or service will be visible, accessible, and convenient to your target audience. In other words, fly with the wind and not against it!

You don't want to open a luxury jewelry shop in a neighborhood where there are only pawnshops, vacant factories, rundown houses, and payday loan offices. Common sense indicates that such an area is experiencing an economic downturn and resident flight. The people who are still there are probably not in the market for a diamond tennis bracelet or a Patek Philippe watch.

Doing research and making sure it's up to date and not from three, five, or ten years ago is crucial. Looking at historic patterns can be helpful in identifying trends and the effect certain other variables may have, but mostly you want current data on consumer habits, income levels, and shopping patterns. You want to know what they read, which restaurants they dine in, where they go to church, where they work, how they dress, and what their problems are that you can fix.

Taking flight with your entrepreneurial dreams takes immense courage. Perhaps the most frightening thing I've ever done was hire employees and risk, not only my business's success, but the livelihood of various individuals and their families. No matter how thorough and promising your research may be, any successful flight plan must include faith. Often there is no safety net. You must feel the fear and do what needs doing anyway. Faith doesn't mean that you ignore facts and figures or discount common sense. Faith needs data in order to see beyond it.

Weather forecasting means considering more than just the immediate vicinity where you want to set up shop. It means looking at the health of the national and international economy as well as personal circumstances and present responsibilities. If you have young children, then you will have to accommodate their presence in your plans, which could mean working from home with them with you, including child care costs in your budget of expenses, or finding creative solutions.

Finally, there will never be a perfect time to take your first step toward launching your new business or entrepreneurial dream. Yes, it's important to have and to develop a keen sense of timing, but even with Swiss-watch precision, you will still make mistakes, get blindsided by the decisions of others, and face unexpected obstacles.

Reading the direction of the wind, personally and professionally, is both art and science. And while I believe that present conditions are optimal for all of us with entrepreneurial passion, I also think some people have an advantage. In other words, if you're a woman and want to soar, the wind is blowing your way!

PART II

BUILD YOUR
WINGS

He gives strength to the weary and increases the power of the weak...those who hope in the LORD will renew their strength. They will soar on wings like eagles....

—Isaiah 40:29–31

CHAPTER 4

It Takes Two

Inspiration and Innovation

The man who has no imagination has no wings.
—Muhammad Ali

I grew up during the Space Age, a period that began with the Russian launch of Sputnik the year I was born. Throughout the 1960s, the race was on as our country competed to be the first to land a manned spacecraft on the moon. Fueled by television shows like *My Favorite Martian*, *The Jetsons*, *Star Trek*, and *Lost in Space*, it seemed every starstruck boy and girl dreamed of being an astronaut like Neil Armstrong or Buzz Aldrin or a futuristic explorer like Captain Kirk, Mr. Spock, or Lieutenant Uhura, one of the only non–white male characters zipping around the galaxy.

In fact, the beloved character portrayed by actress Nichelle Nichols broke boundaries on television simply by featuring a character of African descent in a leadership role rather than one of servitude. In her autobiography, Ms. Nichols reveals that she helped name her character by suggesting the Swahili word for freedom, *uhura*, to series creator Gene Roddenberry. Her character participated in another milestone when she and William Shatner shared one of the earliest interracial kisses on TV, forced to smooch, of course, by hostile aliens encountered on a distant planet.

Even more fascinating than this nostalgic trivia is something Ms. Nichols recently shared in an interview with Neil deGrasse Tyson about why she remained on the show for the duration of its three seasons as well as its transition to feature films (https://www .startalkradio.net/show/a-conversation-with-nichelle-nichols). Coming from a background in musical theater, she planned to leave after the first season but encountered a most unexpected Trekkie at an NAACP fund-raiser—Dr. Martin Luther King!

Apparently Dr. and Mrs. King were big fans of the show, one of the few programs they allowed their children to watch. When Ms. Nichols shared that she planned to exit the program, Dr. King encouraged her to stay, citing her portrayal as a role model in a peaceful, integrated society as important in popular culture. Ms. Nichols stayed and continued boldly going where no black woman had gone before!

Rising Above

I'm sure it would have been much easier for Nichelle Nichols to remain in her comfort zone, performing with such music icons as the great Duke Ellington, with whom she had toured prior to being cast on *Star Trek*. But she longed to stretch her acting abilities and wasn't going to allow societal stereotypes and cultural racism to stop her. She may not have intended to be a pioneer, but pursuing her dream required her to blaze her own trail. It's no surprise then that Mae Jemison, the first African American woman in space, cites Nichols's Lieutenant Uhura as a role model for her own ground-breaking journey aboard the space shuttle *Endeavour*.

Of course, we likely would never have had shows like *Star Trek*, let alone an actual space program that led to the moon landing, without getting off the ground in the first place. When we consider pioneers of aviation, we usually think about brothers Orville and Wilbur Wright shortly after the turn of the twentieth century getting their fixed-wing flying machine off the ground near Kitty Hawk, North Carolina. Or perhaps those of us who are history buffs might imagine Charles Lindbergh flying across the Atlantic Ocean for the first time or female daredevil Amelia Earhart, the first woman to complete the same solo journey.

But there's an earlier story of human flight that captures my imagination, an ancient myth about an ingenious inventor and his daring escape from a dangerous trap of his own making. The story begins on Crete, the largest of the Greek islands, when King Minos hired a brilliant visionary named Daedalus to design and build a fitting royal residence known as the Palace of Knossos, a stunning architectural marvel whose partially restored remains can still be visited today. Daedalus was also asked to design a prison for the king's enemies, and the result was an enormous maze called the labyrinth.

Like many relationships between owners and contractors, the one between Minos and Daedalus soon soured and the crafty craftsman soon found himself, along with his young son, Icarus, imprisoned in the labyrinth he had designed. Knowing the place as well as he did, Daedalus knew they would never find a way out, and even if they did, they were on an island without a boat. So Daedalus came up with another idea—if they couldn't go out they would go up! Creating wings from fallen branches and beeswax, he found a way to exit vertically.

As fantastical as this story may be, I believe most of us can relate to feeling like we're going around in circles, lost in a maze of our own making, unable to find an exit to the life we long to lead.

Instead we feel trapped in tunnels constructed by too many responsibilities and obligations, hemmed in at every turn by circumstances seemingly beyond our control. Some of the obstacles creating the rows of your labyrinth may be personal and related to your role in your family. Other barriers spring up in your professional endeavors as you strive to please bosses focused on the bottom line at companies that may not exist tomorrow.

For some it may be caring for young children as a single parent while juggling a career, a feat that requires balancing two full-time roles in one 24-hour day. Others may be juggling even heavier burdens, forced to become the caretaker for aging parents or a spouse suffering from chronic illness or injury. For that matter, it may be your own health and medical situation that seem to limit your ability to escape your present imprisonment.

In the workplace we see others promoted into jobs we wanted but didn't get for reasons we don't fully understand. We want to finish our degree, maybe even switch careers, but the risk seems too great and the potential payoff too uncertain. Others may have their degree in hand, along with astronomical student loan debt, but no job. Having a degree no longer means a well-paying, satisfying career awaits—if it ever did. This reality is reinforced by the fact that student loans recently topped the trillion-dollar mark (that's twelve zeroes!) while starting salaries remain the same, buying less with cost of living increases factored in.

During such seasons, we do what we have to do, whatever must be done to feed the kids, pay the bills, clean the house, accompany a parent to a doctor's appointment, and care for the rest of the family. While these demands often feel all-consuming, they will only overwhelm us if we resign ourselves to remaining in our current labyrinth for the rest of our lives. Instead, we must allow Daedalus's example to inspire us to see what we can do with the resources at hand. We must keep our entrepreneurial dreams alive by finding a way to express our creative capabilities even within our contemporary confinements.

We must resist the temptation to give up hope and assume that only those people born with the gilded wings of education and financial stability get to fly. Success crafted from our own hands is not only possible but more satisfying for the amount of tears, sweat, and blood we pour into it. And the first step is not looking up and dreaming about flying to the next level. The first step is seeing how far you've already come.

What has gotten you to the point where you are? What skills have you acquired from working at your present place of employment? Even if it's a negative example, meaning you know what you don't want to do when you're a manager or business owner, it's still valuable.

What creative interests appeal to you? Are you always noticing other women's hairstyles, thinking about what would frame someone's face perfectly? Do you love animals and have a natural gift for training them to be obedient? Do your friends always comment on the tapestry art hanging in your hallway, the one you wove from an assortment of old quilting scraps your grandmother gave you?

And before you tell me you don't have any special talents, abilities, or interests, I beg you to think again and reflect on what you loved as a child that you still love today. Sports cars? Books? Gardening? Cooking? Sewing? As you've noticed by the abundance of books and markers in almost any store you go in, even a childhood favorite like coloring has become big business!

Breath in the Body

One of the reasons I'm drawn to the story of Daedalus escaping the labyrinth is because he not only used what he had to craft wings, he used the greatest tool he had, his mind, to realize that what had gotten him there could also get him out of there. We usually call this kind of realization inspiration, that aha! moment when the spark of our imagination catches flame in the tinder of our present circumstances.

Inspiration can come in all kinds of shapes and sizes, and the very thing that inspires one person may not even be noticed by others. The word itself comes from the Latin *inspirare*, meaning to blow or breathe life into something. It's the word we find in Genesis when God creates Adam. "Then the LORD God formed a man from the dust of the ground and breathed into his nostrils the breath of life, and the man became a living being" (Gen. 2:7).

Notice that first God formed the shape, the body, of this man before performing divine CPR and breathing life into him. Many times we feel inspired by a situation or opportunity and attempt to pour our energy into it before we have created a structure to support it. I see people launch a start-up without considering how to manage day-to-day operations or progressive expansion. Then they reach a plateau where it feels like they're on a treadmill with no way to move forward because they lack the infrastructure required for healthy growth.

It's easy to make the mental jump from your love of baking to owning your own bakery. But the very aspects you enjoy most about baking may be what prevents your bakery from becoming a successful business. I've met several women who, like Miss Robbie Montgomery of Sweetie Pie's, love to cook and therefore get inspired to open their own restaurant or catering business. They have the experience, the artistry, and the culinary creativity to produce mouthwatering meals and decadent desserts.

But what they don't have is the business experience needed to market, advertise, and promote their shop. They don't have the administrative or management skills needed to hire the right people for the right roles. They don't have the investment experience to know when to expand seating at their current location, when to look for a larger venue, and when to open a second shop. It's easy to think of inspiration as simply taking the match of something you love and striking it against your present opportunity. But without a candle to light, your flame will quickly burn out, scorching your fingers instead of illuminating your path.

Inspiration must be grounded in the dust you have gathered and shaped into the body of your business before you attempt to breathe life into it. Many times, too, the idea you birth will begin small, much like an infant gestating in its mother's womb. With nourishment and love, the baby grows until it's time to be birthed into the world. From there it becomes a toddler and continues to mature into childhood and then adulthood. Each stage of development takes time and requires the right stimuli in order for healthy growth to be maximized.

Inspiration also remains grounded in the present moment, enough to adapt to changing conditions. You may often start with one idea and realize the real opportunity lies in something you discover accidentally. Numerous successful products have emerged because somewhere in the development process something went wrong or someone made a mistake. For instance, Coca-Cola supposedly began when a pharmacist's assistant spilled soda water into the glass her boss had been using to create a new headache cure. Although some people might testify to its medicinal powers, most of us consider Coke a better beverage to enjoy over ice on a warm afternoon.

The microwave oven came into existence when an engineer at the end of World War II realized the magnetron he was working on as part of a military radar device had melted the candy bar in his pocket. Kids' favorites Play-Doh and Silly Putty were both the result of mistakes research scientists made in pursuit of other formulas. Charles Goodyear once revealed that his tire company's formula for vulcanized rubber had been discovered at random. Pfizer chemists were working on a new medicine to treat heart ailments when they discovered a startling side effect that resulted in Viagra.

So consider the fact that you're not where you want to be or thought you should be a blessing. Instead of clinging tightly to the original goal you had of starting your own bakery, perhaps consider focusing on and experimenting with your bestselling item. Instead of trying to run a traditional bakery that offers pies, cakes, and pastries, narrow your focus and offer only one kind of item, such as chocolate chip cookies. It apparently worked for Mrs. Fields!

Making It New Again

Inspiration is only half of the equation for successful entrepreneurial flight. While you might be able to get off the ground with only this one wing, you wouldn't go far and you would definitely get tired fast. Instead consider the way that innovation can be your second wing working in tandem with inspiration.

Innovation comes from the Latin root *innovare*, which means to make new or to refresh. This concept assumes that something exists as a foundation, a basis, that is then changed in some way to make it new and improved. In other words, inspiration gets you started but doing it your own way alters what you have to offer in a way that brands it as uniquely your own. No one makes cupcakes, earrings, dust mops, or purses the way Hostess, Tiffany, Swiffer, and Louis Vuitton make those items.

Innovation takes a good thing and makes it better by making it your own. This improvement might be recognizing a greater need it can meet or a more effective way of solving a common problem. It might be adding a certain kind of style or enhancing a particular item so that it's more practical, beautiful, or both.

My concern with so much of the innovation we've seen demonstrated in our consumer culture is that it's motivated solely by sales. If people like the filling in Oreo cookies, they will buy a version with twice as much creme filling in the middle. Not to pick on Oreos, and I confess that I rarely go to the grocery store, but the last time I was in the cookie aisle (don't judge me now!) I counted a dozen different Oreo varieties, including pumpkin spice, red velvet, key lime, orange, not to mention traditional vanilla. To me, these variations are not truly innovative—they're simply for the purpose of satisfying consumers who have culinary curiosity.

Innovation does more than change the flavor—it changes the form. Innovation makes lemons into lemonade and transforms tomatoes into ketchup. When I first imagined MegaFest, I envisioned an event that was a hybrid of many different kinds of events and conferences. I wanted it to unite the community, to educate entrepreneurial minds, to inspire people with amazing preachers, speakers, and musicians, and to entertain with wholesome, family-friendly entertainers, singers, and comedians. I wanted MegaFest to have substance but still be fun, to create an experience unlike anything those in attendance had ever experienced.

Over the years, my vision has evolved and grown and been shaped by trial and error and changes in our culture, environment, and economy. As we grew, the event's sheer size became a factor in decision making because we had to find a venue large enough and accessible enough to accommodate hundreds of thousands of people. We had to think practically about parking, shuttles and public transportation, bathrooms, first aid, concessions, and food.

Each time I get with my team and our other partners to

brainstorm a new MegaFest, I want it not only to be better than the last one but unique to where we are now. I learned that some performers improve each time they're invited back and innovate their talk or concert in ways that keep it fresh for guests who have seen them numerous times before. Similarly, the ones who only have one show, one speech, one concert to share are not typically a good fit.

If you can't diversify what you offer, you limit its reception and ability to endure. Innovators are able to adapt and change elements on the fly, seizing an opportunity from what others consider limitations. Even after Daedalus realized he had nowhere to go but up, he still had to come up with the raw material to craft the wings with which to fly. He didn't have feathers, canvas, or metal, but he did have branches and beeswax.

These materials had limitations—a lesson his son, Icarus, found out the hard way.

When Wings Melt

Before they flew out of the labyrinth, Daedalus warned Icarus not to fly too close to the sun, knowing the heat would melt the wax holding their wings in place. Like most children, Icarus allowed his exuberance to eclipse his father's warning and flew too high too fast. I'm sure he was giddy from the thrill of escaping the twists and turns of the torturous maze where they had been trapped. But he allowed his passion to override practicality with disastrous results.

Once his wings began to melt, Icarus began to plummet, and there was little Daedalus could do to save him. Instead of heeding his father's advice and maintaining an altitude that would have sustained his flight, Icarus crashed into the sea and drowned. Both the sea and a nearby island are named for him.

Perhaps now you see how this mythical legend not only inspires us but serves as a cautionary tale about succeeding too quickly. I've seen this happen many times with entrepreneurial endeavors that had plans in place for steady growth and long-term sustainability but no plans for skyrocketing overnight. If you can't ship hundreds of cakes from your online bakery site, then it really doesn't matter how good your cakes are. If you can't handle a production order because you lack the staff to fulfill it, then this missed opportunity can have a ripple effect as word spreads that your operation can only handle small jobs.

I recall a situation in Dallas in which a community development nonprofit launched a small printing company employing many homeless men and women as well as others recently paroled from their incarceration. Wanting to help support this worthy endeavor, I approached the director about printing some promotional merchandise for an upcoming event. Participants at the conference would be receiving gift bags that included pens, pads, mugs, and caps that would all be printed with our logo.

The director was thrilled and appreciated the business, but it became apparent very quickly that her enthusiasm could not make up for the lack of organizational resources required to fulfill our printing order. They kept changing the delivery date until finally we were backed into a corner as the deadline for our event approached. I knew it would be expensive to complete the order at the last minute using another printer, but I also wanted to include the planned materials in the corporate gift bags.

Despite the good intentions and significant donations of many people, this nonprofit venture tried to take on too much too soon without the resources in place to guarantee their product services. I was saddened but not surprised when it dissolved the following year. And I couldn't help but wonder if they had started out slower with fewer people and smaller orders whether they would have grown at a steadier, healthier pace. I also had to wonder if anyone in the organization had experience running a printing business or whether that was chosen based on perceived market need and statistical analytics.

On the other end of the spectrum, I think of a woman I know who was a gifted seamstress. She longed to be a fashion designer and had experience working in women's wear at high-end department stores. While her designs were striking and her tailoring impeccable, the trends and timing never worked in her favor to launch her own label. So she kept making clothes for herself and a handful of friends and paying clients. Then, one day, a client noticed a unique broach she was wearing. Made of old costume jewelry pieces and discarded fabric swatches, the eye-catching ornament was unlike anything the client had ever seen, so she asked the woman to make one for her.

You likely know the rest of the story—this woman discovered a niche market for an artistic creation that hit a nerve with the fickle fashionistas. After she had made and sold a couple dozen of her collage creations, the woman knew that if they caught on, she would be in trouble because she had no supply stockpiled and ready to sell. She was torn about what to do because, on one hand, as an artist only she could imagine, design, and execute these unique adornments.

But on a practical level, this woman saw an opportunity to grow a business if she were willing to let go of her ego. So she enlisted her teenaged daughter, niece, and two of their friends to spend a weekend with her learning to create the one-of-a-kind broaches. The young ladies not only had a knack for assembling these miniature works of art, they began putting their own unique stamp on the process. They started making earrings to match some of the pins, which of course led to necklaces, bracelets, and rings.

When the woman called in favors from friends in the fashion industry, every single one of them loved her collection, and soon she had dozens of items for sale in exclusive boutiques in New York, Chicago, and Los Angeles. She wasted no time employing the young women and also asked them to recruit new hires with similar tastes and talents as their own. She knew that she would always be the creative heartbeat of the venture but that she needed additional team members for her business to become full-bodied.

Fall Out of Your Nest

Even when you have both wings of inspiration and innovation working together to harness the wind beneath them, you will soon discover that it takes practice to fly. If you've ever watched a baby bird hatch in the nest, you know it takes time before it is ready to fly. We once had a pair of mourning doves nesting in a tree outside our bedroom window, and it was like watching the Discovery Channel in 3-D. Many details of the parental relationship struck me as I learned that these doves mate for life. This pair had three eggs that soon hatched into a trio of ugly little balls of gray fuzz with hungry beaks always open.

In a few days they matured and began looking more like birds and not lint from the dryer. Then one morning I noticed the biggest chick perched on the edge of the nest while its siblings watched from below. I assumed it would be only a matter of moments before he flew away, but it actually turned out to be another entire day. He would stretch his wings, hop to a nearby branch, jump back to the edge of the nest, and then repeat the process. It was like watching a kid on the diving board above a swimming pool, wanting to jump but fearful and uncertain at the same time.

The next day I noticed he had flown to a branch several feet higher while watching his brother and sister climb to the edge of the nest to repeat the process he had just completed. One of them followed suit quickly and joined him on an upper branch. The third, however, was in no hurry, and when she seemed to lose her balance and topple over the edge, fluttering like a leaf to the ground below, I feared she might not survive. But then I saw her pop up from the lawn below, make a running start, and begin flapping with all her might.

It was both comical and heartbreaking as I watched her try and fail to get off the ground. But finally, after many attempts, this little bird caught the breeze and flew back up to the nest where her family was waiting. Within moments, all five flew the coop, leaving nothing behind except an empty nest and that mournful song for which they are known.

That was the last day we saw the birds, but what an up-close, fascinating process I had been privileged to witness! And the big lesson for me was about patience, perseverance, and practice. I'm sure I was simply projecting and personifying these young doves as they learned to do what God created them to do, but I was so inspired by their journey to flight that I returned to a project that I had put on hold indefinitely.

It was a film project that had never come together with the right script, the right director, or enough backing. Nonetheless, the story captivated me and I sensed it would be one with broad appeal to many young adults and families with children. Along with several other production partners, I had tried repeatedly to align the right creative team as well as the needed resources to ensure an adequate budget for postproduction and distribution. With the image of that little bird still in mind, I reopened the file, reviewed my notes on the script, and tried to think about other ways to produce the film.

Then, suddenly, it seemed so clear. Instead of a feature film, what if it were the pilot for a limited-run series on one of the many providers of online entertainment such as Hulu, Netflix, or Amazon? This sent me in an entirely different direction as I thought through how to expand the cast to a full ensemble and extend the plot into several longer story arcs. With this new direction in mind, I then made a couple of phone calls and discovered that others loved my idea and agreed to support it.

We'll see if the pilot gets picked up for a full slate of episodes, but even if it doesn't, I consider this project wildly successful because of the way it started in one form and evolved into another. My friends who are artists, actors, and writers tell me this is quite common and is in fact the secret to successful improvisation. In order to keep the improv alive, performers learn early on the secret to doing it successfully: letting go of their own expectations about what the performance should be and saying yes to whatever opportunity their collaborators present to them. One of them told me, "Staying engaged and actually listening—instead of being in my head and anticipating what I should say next—is the hardest part."

I suspect the same is true for entrepreneurs trying to get a new venture off the ground. We must not only be attuned to our own avenues and abilities but also to ways we can make them our own unique creation, one that's sustainable for flight over a long distance. It won't be easy, and even after we rise above the labyrinth of labors pulling at us in all directions, we must remain vigilant and not allow the rush of success to push us too near the sun.

No matter your circumstances, I challenge you to rise above them and in fact use them to free yourself to get to the stratosphere where you belong. If you allow yourself to remain perched on the edge of life's nest, afraid to test your wings, then you risk missing out on becoming the person God made you to be. Chances are good that you will free-fall and struggle to get to your feet before stretching your wings again. But if you're willing to keep trying, you will soon discover the exhilaration that comes from creating an enterprise that can soar.

CHAPTER 5

Flight Plan

Your Blueprint for Success

Good fortune is what happens when opportunity meets with planning.

—Thomas Edison

My family and friends sometimes tease me about the way I like to build a sermon around fresh interpretations of Scripture using surprising metaphors or unexpected examples. They know I like a challenge and that I want my preaching, teaching, and speaking to be as relevant, engaging, powerful, and transformative to my audience as possible. In other words, I don't want people falling sleep while I'm talking!

Many people compliment me on both my content and my style of delivery, telling me how natural, even effortless, I make it look to speak in front of thousands of people. I share this with you not to brag about my ability or blow my own horn, because God certainly gets all the glory for inspiring my messages and using them in people's lives. It would be erroneous, however, for you to assume that I don't prepare, read, research, pray, and organize my thoughts ahead of time.

You see, I'm convinced preparation facilitates liberation. My mind is naturally curious so I find myself reading, meditating, making notes, and researching far longer than you might expect. I've never been to seminary, but I've studied the Bible since I was a boy. And as corny as it may sound, I really enjoy being a student of human nature and a keen observer of the world around me. Learning stimulates me and serves as a catalyst for the opportunities when I am blessed to share what I've learned with others.

While preparation is crucial for me, I also want the freedom to customize my message extemporaneously for the specific audience hearing it and the context in which they are receiving it. Never wanting to sound scripted or contrived, I discovered early in my pastoral career that the key to keep it real and sound natural is to do all the work ahead of time and commit it to paper. In order to improvise or adjust my points on the fly, I need to have adequate preparation and support beneath the surface of my delivery. I need to have my main point in mind—my destination, where I want to take my audience— and how I'm going to get us there—my transportation, the examples and ideas supporting my main point.

The same is true for any journey, whether it's physical, spiritual, intellectual, or emotional—and it's absolutely essential to launch a successful business. Whether getting from point A to point B in a sermon or in the Sahara, you need a flight plan!

Up in the Air

Rarely does anyone ride in an airplane just for the experience of flying. As amazing as the view is or as tasty as those peanuts and pretzels might be, virtually no one buys a plane ticket for those benefits. No; passengers pay money for a seat on an airplane to get to a specific destination. When I hop on a flight at DFW Airport, I'm going somewhere for a specific purpose—to shoot a show in Los Angeles, to speak in Atlanta, to meet with new partners in New York. I don't fly just to count the clouds for two or three hours, and neither do you!

Similarly, you are launching a new venture to get somewhere, and your destination is what we typically call success. So don't be afraid to admit that you want to succeed! You surely don't want to pour all your heart, soul, sweat, and tears—not to mention your dollars—into a venture just for the fun of seeing what it will do. Your business is your baby, something you've dreamed about and created. Like a good parent, you want your infant venture to grow and mature and become a vibrant, healthy business.

Scripture reminds us that "hope deferred makes the heart sick, but a longing fulfilled is a tree of life" (Prov. 13:12). You don't want to plant something only to watch it wither and die before it bears fruit. You want a strong sapling that grows into your sturdy tree of life. You don't want your flying machine to hover just above the tree line—you want to reach 30,000 feet.

Obviously, anyone who starts a business wants the business to be a viable source of economic empowerment and profitability. But profitability isn't accomplished by watching the bottom line alone. It's equally important that one of your barometric indicators require that the consumer has had the best experience possible with the process and with product quality. Both marketing cost and sustainability are more easily achieved when the customer's needs are very high in your priority list. If that goal is achieved, the business by virtue of quality experiences will sell itself!

Keep in mind, however, that your destination is not just about dollars. Success is not merely defined by your profit margin, although your profitability will likely determine your sustainability, which is also an essential part of success. Most people want to create a business that they can either sell for a considerable profit or leave as a legacy for their heirs. You want to make a contribution to your own future as well as the future of younger generations coming along behind you.

With success as your destination, you're finally ready to draft a flight plan for the nuts and bolts of your new venture. You've already studied weather patterns and wind speeds and learned about the environment where your business will live. You've identified your problem to solve and know something about who you want to target as your customers. Now you need to put all your insight, inspiration, and information into one document that can serve as your master plan.

Before you build a viable business in your life, you must build it in your head. And because lots of other ideas and distractions will compete for space in your brain, you must commit your flight plan to writing. When you first begin this process, it will be like thinking out loud on paper or on your device's screen—adding, changing, erasing, revising, refining. Business plans not only tell others—as well as yourself, which is often more valuable than you realize when you're putting it together—what your plane looks like and where it's going, but they also tell how you're going to get there.

I'm always shocked at the number of entrepreneurs wanting my advice or an investment in their venture who look at me funny when I ask to see their business plan. Most of them tell me it's all in their head, which I can appreciate but cannot see! While I know that sometimes events happen quickly and you begin your business before you intended to, or for some fortunate few the business seems to fall in your lap, you still need to establish some kind of business plan if you want to reach your destination: success, defined as both profitability and sustainability over time.

Think of the job of an architect. She doesn't begin her new building with actual materials. Her job is to deliver a design that diminishes problems on paper. She studies weight loads, heating concerns, functionality, and aesthetics. The purpose of the architect is to produce a design that has considered the weight, the pressure, the strength, the environment, and other usage factors that would lead to a successful structure. If you plan it right with a pencil, you can build it right with steel. Pencils are easier to correct than welding!

Your business plan is just as important as an architect's blueprint. Your plan is both essential and valuable because anyone seriously willing to consider investing their resources is unlikely to do so if you haven't invested time and energy into drawing out a design that anticipates the inevitability of the challenges ahead. Potential investors want to see the extent to which you've envisioned the future as you attempt to reach your destination.

Keep in mind that each business plan is unique and should reflect your particular field or industry, your personal passion and professional advantages, and your constituents' sensibilities. While numerous templates exist for basic business plans, one size does not fit all, so use them as guides to craft your own.

Your business plan must be customized to your industry, field, and audience. A plan for launching a neighborhood beauty salon will look different from a plan for starting a technical consulting business and from a plan for selling your hand knitting online. Similar to the way you might adjust a résumé, this customization should be as specific as possible to your particular venture.

There are all kinds of business plans, ranging in length from one page to some that are longer than this book. Numerous resources are available, with models emphasizing different aspects of your plan over others, and I recommend a few of my favorites in the Appendix. I encourage you to study a variety of them and pick and choose the best for your business. Whether you want only a bare-bones skeleton for your plan, a more full-bodied elaboration, or something in between, all business plans should remain works in progress that can be studied and updated often.

To get you started, I suggest answering the following questions in writing without worrying about spelling, grammar, or perfecting your prose. Just write out your responses in a sentence or two, knowing that some may require additional research or reflection upon revision. As you can see, there's nothing magical about these questions—I've basically just used the old reporter's trick of looking at a story from all angles. My hope is that answering these queries will provide you with the raw material to draft your design for ultimate success.

YOUR *SOAR!* FLIGHT PLAN

WHAT?

What are you selling? What problem are you solving?
What's your mission and motivation?
What makes your business unique?
What's your destination? What will success look like for your business?

WHO?

Who needs what you want to offer? Who's your ideal customer?
Who else could use your product or service?

Who will be on your support team? Who are the other professionals you need to consult or hire for their expertise? Lawyers? Accountants? Consultants? Others?

Who might want to invest in your business?

WHY?

Why do people need your product or service?

Why should they buy it from you instead of from one of your competitors?

Why will they return to your business and refer others to you?

Why will you succeed where other, similar businesses have failed?

HOW?

How will you operate? How will you handle production, distribution, delivery, etc.?

How much money do you need to get started? How will you raise this capital?

How will you market and promote your business?

How will you manage cash flow?

WHERE?

Where is your airspace, the ideal atmosphere where your business will succeed?

Where will your business be located physically?

Where will potential customers learn about what you're offering?

Where do you want your business to be three years from now?

WHEN?

When will you start your business? What specific season and date make sense?

When will you know your venture is a success? When you serve a certain number of customers? Make a certain percentage margin of profit? Reach sales of a certain number or range?

When will you need to rescale your business? Hire more employees? Move to a larger location?

When will you consider selling your business?

Another Way to Get There

Perhaps you don't like all these questions and don't particularly enjoy writing long, detailed responses. If so, I suggest finding another way to create your business plan—perhaps visually with graphics, charts, and pictures. Maybe you put it together as a slide show you can present to prospective customers and investors, something you can use or build from for your new website. If you're an artist, you might create your own quirky flow chart, cartoon, or painting that specifically illustrates the big ideas for your business.

Depending on your unique variables, you might consider making a video that can be posted to YouTube or recording a podcast, perhaps with help from someone you know who already has a following. While these creative expressions may strike you as more a matter of marketing and promotion, if done well they can provide all the specific information one usually finds in a formal, written business plan. Personally, I recommend that you do what works best for you—and then make sure you have something in writing that you can post, text, tweet, email, or hand to customers and investors.

If you choose one of these more creative expressions for your business plan, here are the major categories you should consider addressing: an overview of your mission (often called an executive summary); a description of atmospheric conditions in the airspace where you hope to fly, the state of business currently in your chosen sector; market analysis and competitive strategies; operational logistics; financials; and your destination, the way you will know you've met certain goals or metrics. Let's briefly consider each of these ingredients.

Overview of Your Mission

Also known more formally as an executive summary, this sets the tone for both your business and the rest of your business plan. This information provides the first impression readers receive about you and your business. It's usually a paragraph or two and addresses most of the "WHAT?" questions directly while touching on "WHO?" and "WHY?" as well. It indicates the specific legal form of operation you have chosen—a sole proprietorship, partnership, corporation, or limited liability company (LLC). If you're unfamiliar with these terms, please refer to the Appendix for a brief definition of each one.

This overview of your mission should be direct and tightly focused. This is not the place for creative marketing language and over-the-top sales copy. You want to be taken seriously and have your business clearly identified and accurately described, highlighting its unique distinction within the competitive marketplace where it will fly. Again, I encourage you to do some research and peruse a variety of business plans and their executive summaries to see what you think will work best for your venture.

Atmospheric Conditions

Like a good weather forecaster, you should be able to give a concise description of your chosen business sector's current conditions. This section addresses the "WHERE?" questions while touching on your answers for "WHO?" and "WHEN?" If you can place these current conditions within a specific context, then all the better. Depending on your field, you may want to note certain patterns or the kinds of "storm fronts" that tend to move through your airspace. Providing this overview should show why now is a good time to launch your business. Or if not, then you will need to address how you will fly against the wind at takeoff.

From this general assessment of business conditions, you should then narrow the funnel to a more specific description and explanation of where your business will attempt to fly. What's the economic mood in the neighborhood where your dress shop will be located? What's the average age of residents you hope to reach in your targeted ten-mile radius around your restaurant? When is the ideal date to launch your holiday catering service? Answering these kinds of questions shows that you're well aware of the weather you're about to fly into.

Market Analysis and Competitive Strategies

This section focuses on the habits and histories of your customers and your competition. It addresses many of the "HOW?" and some of the "WHY?" questions. Here you summarize what your research has revealed about the market you want to penetrate with your product or service. What's the size of this market? Its rate of growth? How is it organized or structured? What are its unique, even idiosyncratic, features? What are the latest trends in this market? How often have trends tended to shift? How will your business address this market in light of all these variables?

And perhaps more importantly, how will your business be able to compete in this market and who are the major players you're up against? Who's the Goliath you're up against? What are the strengths and weaknesses of your competitors? Why is your business going to be able to compete with these opponents? While it's tempting to think your product, service, or business is the first of its kind, most for-profit entities have some competition—if not from a similar product or service, then from something or someone pulling potential customers' attention and assets away from you.

Operational Logistics

This section gets to the nitty-gritty of the "HOW?" questions. It provides a sequential schedule for design, production, delivery, distribution, and point of sale for your product or service. In addition, try to describe the way you envision your business running on a daily basis. Will you hire employees? How many? What will their roles and responsibilities be in terms of the operational process? Forgive me for sounding like one of those old vinyl record players stuck in the same groove, but be as specific as you can in thinking about the life of your product or service from inception to birth to maturation.

Financials

You will likely answer the rest of the "HOW?" questions not already covered as you address financials for your business. While this may be a new or murky area for you, I cannot emphasize enough or overstate its importance. Learning about the financial components your business requires may necessitate consultation with other professionals—accountants, lawyers, lenders, investors, consultants, and other established professionals in your sector.

Consider your business's start-up requirements and where, and from whom, this capital will come. You will want to draft an income statement and project how your business will establish profitability. Cash flow is one of the biggest problems for new businesses so you definitely want to spend some time considering how you will fund operations if your projected profits are not realized on time. Many businesses have seasonal cycles they follow, times that are more profitable for various reasons as well as times when operating and production costs are higher or lower. Identifying these cycles ahead of time will save you countless headaches, not to mention all kinds of sleepless nights!

Your Destination

Finally, you will want to identify some specific ways you will know when your business has arrived at its destination of successful, sustained flight. Many business owners base this not only on profit margins but on growing their customer base, expanding public awareness, and enduring for a particular time period such as five or ten years. Not only will establishing these goals before you're airborne help you know where you're going, they will assist you in making decisions about growth, product expansion, target marketing, and more.

Knowing your destination is also helpful in identifying when you need to make changes in the business. Because even if you're able to remain in the air, your plane may be losing velocity or even some of its parts! If you've anticipated how your business will mature and what it will need to grow at a healthy rate, you can avoid the stress that often sends entrepreneurs plummeting to the ground. Curiously enough, the unexpected success of a young business can be just as taxing and stressful—perhaps more so—than the lack of projected sales. In either case, a good business plan will help you know what you need before you need it, reducing your stress levels along the way.

The Weight of Your Success

I learned this lesson about anticipating stress the hard way, but over time I've recognized what works for me. In fact, I recently spoke at a business conference sponsored by *SUCCESS* magazine about an event from my boyhood that has become a tragic symbol of stress left unchecked.

When I was growing up in Charleston, West Virginia, there was a bridge about sixty miles northwest up US Highway 35 known as the Silver Bridge. It had been built in the 1920s and spanned the Ohio River, facilitating travel between the Mountain State and the Buckeye State. If we went to visit relatives in that area, we would have to go over the Silver Bridge, which seemed enormous to me as a child.

On December 15, 1967—I would've been ten years old—the Silver Bridge collapsed right at rush hour. In less than a minute, more than thirty vehicles fell into the cold river, killing forty-six of the sixty-four people on board (Jim Henry, "Pike's Past," www.news watchman.com/blogs/pikes_past/article_2bf5283b-c086-53e7 -bb85-6a824e824d82.html). After the victims' bodies were recovered, government engineers studied the ruins of the structure that had provided safe passage for almost forty years. They discovered that despite how solid the Silver Bridge appeared, it had been supporting more weight than it was intended to bear for some time. This strain apparently led to a stress fracture, which along with hidden corrosion caused the bridge's collapse. Finally, it could no longer support the thousands of pounds of rubber and steel traversing its suspended lanes.

The tragedy shocked us all and garnered national attention, including assurance from President Johnson that the bridge would be rebuilt with federal support. Obviously, this event made a lasting impression on me, both for the terrible loss of life it caused but also for the reason behind the bridge's collapse. I recall overhearing some people talking about how the bridge had been constructed at a time when automobiles were still relatively new and fairly light compared to the larger, heavier sedans and trucks of our own time. Consequently, the bridge was bearing more weight than it was intended to carry, without additional structural support. But no one realized this until, sadly, it was too late and dozens of lives had been lost.

In recent years, I often think of the Silver Bridge whenever I begin to feel stressed in my own life. When my schedule gets crazy and various responsibilities begin to overlap, naturally my stress level tends to rise. During these times, my wife usually tells me to take a vacation in order to relax and rejuvenate. This remedy works for her and so she assumes it works for me.

I've discovered, however, that when I take a vacation solely to de-stress, I usually feel even more stressed when I return. Not only are my thoughts preoccupied with problems for much of my time away, but the source of my stress is still there waiting on me to return. I haven't resolved the problem—I've only delayed it!

Eventually, I learned a different way to alleviate my stress. My aha! moment came when I realized being stressed is not just about burnout and depleted energy levels. The real source of the stress is the increased weight added by new roles and responsibilities as well as unexpected conflicts and complications. *Stress is about lacking the structural support for the weight you're carrying.* It's about carrying too much additional, unplanned baggage for too long.

As soon as I had this realization, I began adding more organizational strength to the load-bearing areas of my life. I began revising my business plans and rethinking what I need to sustain the flight of my various ventures. I found hiring the right person to whom I can delegate the source of my stress better than any trip to the beach.

Your business plan is the foundation for avoiding stress in your life. It provides you with a rudder that can adjust to the harshest winds as well as a compass to help steer your plane into smoother airspace. Your plan will need frequent updates, tweaks, and revisions as you maintain flexibility and adapt to changing environmental conditions. If the Silver Bridge had been modernized with additional support beams, perhaps it would not have collapsed under the increased weight load.

While it's too late to change the Silver Bridge's tragic fate, you can prevent your business from collapsing down the road. You can design your business plan to accommodate shifts in the amount of weight it must carry. You can make sure the connection between product and customer remains strong enough to bear increased traffic.

With a powerful business plan, you can build a bridge to carry the weight of your success.

Use What You've Got

As you assemble your flight plan, the idealist in you may be tempted to hold out for optimal conditions and the perfect runway to give your new venture the very best opportunity to succeed. While I encourage you to do all you can to set yourself up for success, I would also caution you not to let your idealism provide excuses that delay your start. While you definitely want to make sure there's wind beneath your wings and customers for what you're selling, you will never have perfect conditions that can guarantee your success with certainty. Market conditions will always have a certain volatility. Competition will always threaten your success. Nonetheless, you've got to use what you've got and make the most of it!

Keep in mind the first airplane was built in a less than ideal environment, not in a giant hangar or cavernous garage. The Wright brothers' early prototypes for their flying machine were built in their bicycle shop in Dayton, Ohio. Obviously, Wilbur and Orville knew they weren't trying to build a bicycle! But they also knew that the ideal environment for what they were building didn't exist yet. They were blazing a trail and breaking new ground so there was no perfect laboratory for their construction. Working in their own bicycle shop, however, provided them with most of the necessary raw ingredients: tools and tires, wood and metal, nuts and bolts.

Similarly, you don't have to have everything you'd ideally like to have in order to get started. Instead, use what you have to get to what you don't. Start-ups seldom start perfectly and often resemble the beginning of a marriage—making adjustments and accommodations for the new dynamic of being together as a couple. In the beginning, the Wright brothers' early aircraft model was under-powered and difficult to steer. It lurched and sputtered, popped and pinged, but it didn't take to the air.

They moved forward by always learning from each attempt. Even when it seemed that they were taking two steps back for every step forward, Orville and Wilbur kept copious notes and then discussed, argued, and brainstormed their way to their next adjustment (David McCullough, *The Wright Brothers*, Simon & Schuster, 2015). They assumed they wouldn't get the wings right the first time or have the accurate angle of ascent for takeoff versus landing. They knew it was all part of the process. Whatever frustration, impatience, anger, and disappointment they experienced as years passed without their model taking off was mitigated by the momentum of moving toward that moment when they were suspended above the ground.

Expecting some dysfunction throughout your process also helps you modify your expectations. A strong business plan anticipates and addresses such potential pitfalls and their resolutions. The first plane didn't glide like an eagle, nor was it quiet as a sparrow. Though the movement of birds inspired it, the first attempts didn't function with the grace and ease of a falcon—it was more like the fits and starts of trying to get an enormous kite off the ground.

One of the most important things for an entrepreneur to know is that your business may not proceed down the runway and into the air according to the way you describe it in your business plan. Start-ups often have to sputter their way into the air. You may have to sell pound cakes online to virtual customers before you discover that the sweet spot of opportunity for you is actually opening a bricks-and-mortar bakery in your own neighborhood.

Mistakes, errors, and disappointments are necessary ingredients, so don't pressure yourself for perfection or criticize yourself for not knowing everything prior to the moment when you make a mistake. It is what's wrong with the business that gives you the experience you need to get it right. Working through dysfunction is a factor you must include in the plan. Don't try to avoid it because you can't—and better yet, you don't want to avoid it. *You want to learn from it.*

Smooth Landings

At the time I'm writing this, a couple of major airlines are suffering public criticism over a handful of situations exposed by social-media-savvy passengers. They, too, are trying to learn from their mistakes. In each instance, the airlines' first response has been to defend their crew members' handling of these situations by reminding us of their policies.

In our post 9/11 world where the potential for devastating acts of terrorism seems to lurk around every corner, airlines have implemented strict guidelines and policies to ensure the safety of passengers and crew members. While such measures are both justifiable and understandable, they also overlap and sometimes infringe on the rights and expectations of paying customers. As a result, many of the stringent rules and regulations are being reexamined to avoid more customer-relations debacles while ensuring safety for all involved.

These incidents remind us that having a plan that anticipates problems is essential; otherwise, each situation would end up being treated subjectively, inconsistently, and even arbitrarily. But these incidents also emphasize the necessity of listening to and incorporating customer feedback and then updating our plans. For several decades we heard "the customer is always right" as a mantra for ensuring the success of a business. While this statement still holds merit, you want to be careful because customer demands can smother you if you attempt to cater to every whim, critique, and request a customer makes.

The key is to listen but not necessarily to act. Remember, most passengers aren't pilots! They don't know how to fly your plane because only you can determine what changes to make and how and when to make them. Business plans, like flight plans, must remain flexible so your business can adapt to unexpected situations in real time. Without them, you risk flying by the seat of your pants, literally, all the time—an exhausting prospect to say the least. In other words, indulge me once more as I stress the vital importance of crafting a written plan for your business. Consider it an ongoing work in progress as well as a basis of comparison between the reality of your business and the vision you cast for its success.

Finally, I must confess to you that I have not always drafted a written business plan for every single venture or entrepreneurial endeavor I've launched in my lifetime. And there have been times when I've been humbled by experience for not having one! But whether I have it in my head or in an eighty-page prospectus, I've always tried to work with the end in mind so that I can work backward to see what steps need to be taken.

Like the leaders I admire and seek to emulate, I try to look ahead not only at what's probably going to be next but also what other possibilities and contingencies might pop up along the way. Such preparation, like the groundwork before I speak or preach, often goes unseen or unused, but it gives me the freedom to ensure a smooth landing! *Preparation facilitates liberation.*

While I believe preparation is never wasted, I pray some of the information I share in this chapter will provide high-octane fuel for your engine. Use your business plan, my friend, to make sure you not only take off and soar to new heights but also so that you know how and when to land and take off again. A good business plan is indispensable and increases the odds of your success by leaps and bounds. If you want to see nothing but blue sky, then make sure your flight plan is in black and white!

CHAPTER 6

Invisible Wings

Riding the Winds of E-Commerce

We see our customers as invited guests to a party and we are the hosts.

—Jeff Bezos, founder of Amazon

N o one loves Christmas more than my wife, Serita. One of the most generous and loving people you will ever meet, she relishes making the holiday season both holy and happy for her family, friends, and church family. From decorations with fresh evergreens, holly, and candles to delicious sweets and inviting smells of cinnamon and peppermint from her kitchen, she loves attending to the details that define our celebration.

And my wife definitely speaks the love language of gift giving as she delights in surprising me, along with our kids and grandkids, with thoughtful, personal presents that hit the bull's-eye almost every time. It might be an alligator-skin belt for me, silver suede boots for one of our daughters, or the latest gadget for the grandkids. Regardless of the recipient, her beautifully wrapped boxes with festive paper and colorful ribbons contain just what we wanted—even if we didn't know we wanted it!

But one exception to the joyful season typically transformed my Mrs. Claus into a grumpy Grinch: *Christmas shopping*. Those two words filled my heart with dread as I knew they would leave my spouse stressed and stretched. Although she loves people and creating magical events, my beautiful wife is an introvert who needs downtime to recharge. In the midst of the holiday madness and overflowing schedule, she would rush from the mall to the toy shop, from the electronics store to the fashion boutique.

Even when the children or I helped, holiday shopping was still overwhelming. As much as Serita loves giving the perfect gifts, she used to hate the crowded stores, long lines, and scavenger hunts for the soon-to-be-sold-out item on someone's list. It left her exhausted and frustrated and often cast a shadow on her otherwise starlit holiday.

Then everything changed.

This past Christmas, for example, I recall sitting beside my wife at home watching a movie in early December. Noticing that she kept typing on her phone, I asked if she was texting someone or playing a game. She looked up at me smiling and said, "Oh, no—I just finished my Christmas shopping!"

Putting the *E* in Easy

Like millions of others, particularly during the holiday season, my wife has discovered the utter convenience of shopping online. No lines, no crowds, no hustle and bustle from store to store. Just a few scrolls on a given site followed by a few clicks to place an order. And a few days later, there's a package on the doorstep. E-commerce puts the *e* in easy!

E-commerce can be particularly attractive to those who want to subsidize their existing income or individuals who need to be at home with ailing parents or warming baby bottles for a newborn. For many parents with special-needs children, e-commerce gives a chance for creativity and income while making them available for those they love.

You'll miss a lot if you're trying to decide whether to open a bricks-and-mortar business or go with e-commerce. It isn't always an either or proposition. Many who run a business don't have time to create a satellite store beyond their physical location. So offering your goods and services online may be a great way to do both.

The benefits are numerous. You can link social media to your online storefront or website and remain open all the time for people around the world. There is no other way to be open twenty-four hours around the world and service customers with products, seminars, or exercise training while you are still in your pj's drinking hot chocolate! The minimal cost is also a strong feature in flattening out the playing field and incorporating a much more attainable business model—no need for office space, leases, insurance, and payroll taxes!

No wonder then that e-commerce—the selling, buying, and transacting of business online—has become the fastest growing segment of our economy in recent years. In fact, total e-commerce sales were estimated to be just shy of $400 billion dollars for 2016, which was an increase of more than 15 percent from the previous year. Overall retail sales were up by roughly 3 percent, with e-commerce sales accounting for about 8 percent (www.census.gov/retail/mrts /www/data/pdf/ec_current.pdf, accessed May 1, 2017).

And in case you don't think of yourself as a numbers person, please allow me to translate: e-commerce offers *huge* opportunities for entrepreneurs, and there's plenty of room to grow! For starters, just consider how much has changed in your own lifetime. Are you old enough to even remember a time when you didn't shop online?

Or are you like me and can remember the stark contrast between the old ways and the new ways?

I've always been an "early adapter" of technology, but some cultural changes and advancements are easier to assimilate than others. For example, consider the ways that the Internet has changed not only retail but also communication, entertainment, sports—and even church! We learned very quickly how many viewers connected with The Potter's House via their computer, and we worked to make our resources—sermons, events, messages, books, music, and prayer support—available to them in this new dimension.

We didn't have to invest in our website and the technology required to facilitate building an online community. We could have remained a bricks-and-mortar church focused only on the needs of the congregation that participated here in Dallas. But if we had put our heads down and focused only on the floor in our sanctuary, then we would have missed the incredible opportunities we have to serve, bless, educate, and inspire millions of people around the world. Having frequently traveled around the globe to speak and minister, I knew many people longed to learn more about God and to connect with other kindred souls.

Sometimes, however, new opportunities produce unexpected changes in direction. For instance, our church is now in the midst of a $25 million building program to enlarge our facilities and serve young families. We realized the need not only from the number of young families actively participating in our services but in the feedback, comments, and connection provided by thousands through social media. As a result, we understood the need to adjust our plane's wingspan in midflight!

You see, when I was growing up, there was no such thing as "children's church" or "youth programs." Our church was small and intergenerational. Kids sat in the main service along with their siblings, parents, and grandparents. Special attention to children may have been given at Christmas and Easter, but mostly we children knew we had to pay attention, or at least remain quiet, in order to avoid our mother's angry glare from the choir or a swat on our backsides from our father later.

Now, though, parents want and need time to worship, learn, and grow as adults, without the distraction of young voices and fidgety feet. Single parents especially need relief and time to be spiritually nurtured and nourished. Today's parents also want their children to enjoy time with other children as they learn about God and the Bible through fun activities, games, and age-appropriate music and teaching. With the number of children we're blessed to have at our church, this kind of focus requires dedicated facilities and resources, including the latest audiovisual technology and computer capabilities.

I never imagined being at this stage of my ministry, having served and preached and led for more than four decades, and undertaking a building expansion. But I quickly realized if we didn't move with the cultural current, brought about both by technology and the needs of today's families, we would become irrelevant and underserve our community. We would lose the opportunity to influence the next generation for good. It was a risk I wasn't willing to take.

Nor should you be willing to risk ignoring the impact e-commerce has had on the global landscape. I consider e-commerce a crucial part of any new entrepreneur's business plan, one that must be addressed, assessed, and expressed! Whether you start your business online or use Internet orders to supplement retail sales in your place of business (often called "bricks and clicks"), you cannot afford to ignore e-commerce, nor should you overlook its ability to tap and sustain a global market.

Use It or Lose It

While e-commerce has forever changed the way we do business, I'm still frequently surprised how many entrepreneurs approach me who have shied away from taking their business online. And it seems most of them tend toward extreme ends of the spectrum. The ones who are baby boomers often remain in denial about the way the Internet has dramatically redefined business as we've known it. They may be afraid of technology and consider themselves incapable of learning how to interact with it and benefit from its vast resources. As someone who frequently needs assistance with downloads, uploads, and every load in between, let me assure you that you're not alone!

Nonetheless, you must not allow your lack of expertise or experience to thwart your electronic education. I encourage you to be open and honest about your reluctance even as you push through your hesitancy and learn a new language and a new paradigm for how to do business. Numerous resources are available, many of them free, and you will likely benefit from exposure to a variety of teachers: books, articles, videos, online demos, and good old-fashioned one-on-one tutoring sessions.

Don't be surprised to discover that your best teachers may be your grandchildren, nieces, nephews, or elementary school kids in your neighborhood! They may be more than half your age, but most are usually willing to share their up-to-the-nanosecond expertise and appreciate being asked. Swallow your pride if you have to but do not put off learning fluency with online capabilities. As the kids say, "Use it or lose it!"

At the other end of the spectrum, I often find millennials and younger entrepreneurs taking e-commerce for granted and reacting against it. Most of them grew up with the Internet, email, texting, and social media as part of their everyday lives. As a result, they may long for more authentic contact than online sales allow. "E-commerce used to be one person selling something to another," one told me, "but now it's all about Amazon and other online giants. It's so impersonal—and besides, I can't compete with them." In this backlash to technology and e-commerce, many of these entrepreneurs are opening local businesses that specialize in personal attention, unique experiences, and community service.

As with most things at the extremes, you miss out on what's in the middle if you don't respect the social, cultural, and economic impact e-commerce has had—and will continue to have—on our lives. Just consider the consequences for businesses like Blockbuster, Borders, and Circuit City that failed to adjust to their e-competition, along with thousands of other businesses focused on books, music, and entertainment. Even if you decide to forgo e-commerce in the initial stage of getting your business off the ground, make it a well-informed, deliberate decision, not one made by default.

This chapter will provide you with the fundamental variables you must consider for e-commerce—particularly ways to test the weather conditions before you take flight—along with considerations for additional exploration. My hope is that you will recognize the vast frontier open to your entrepreneurial endeavors thanks to e-commerce and venture forth as a pioneer-for-profit. The process begins, of course, with focusing and clarifying your product as seen from your consumer's computer screen.

The Golden Rule

While e-commerce was already being conducted at a basic level, most experts consider 1994 its seminal year. Not only did Jeff Bezos start his juggernaut e-retailer Amazon (so named because he wanted customers to find everything they needed from A to Z), but 1994 was also the year Marc Andreessen developed the technology for encrypting purchase data, thus enabling online credit card transactions to be made securely and confidently.

The other giant of online retail, and one with which you're most certainly familiar, was birthed two years later by a young Iranian American named Pierre Omidyar. In later interviews he explained, "I started eBay as an experiment, as a side hobby basically, while I had my day job....People were doing business with one another through the Internet already, through bulletin boards. But, on the Web, we could make it interactive, we could create an auction, we could create a real marketplace. And that's really what triggered my imagination, if you will, and that's what I did" (successsshiva .blogspot.com/2012/01/pierre-omidyar-founder-and-chairman .html).

Notice that Mr. Omidyar had no idea he was launching a runaway retail rocket; he was simply following his own curiosity and exploring this new frontier known as the World Wide Web. Since its founding, eBay has become synonymous with online retail, serving as a platform for thousands of e-commerce entrepreneurs around the world. It has maintained strict standards for both its merchants and customers, and this commitment to consistent quality, both in merchandise and in the transaction experience, remains crucial to its ongoing success.

Whether it was from Amazon, eBay, or an established retailer such as Walmart or Sears, you probably remember hitting the button on your computer that finalized your first e-purchase. Do you remember the thrill of sitting there in your pajamas or yoga pants, sipping your cup of coffee, and buying something that wasn't actually in front of you? For myself and so many people I know, it was like something out of science fiction! It was akin to that sensation when we launched rockets into outer space and landed on the moon. Suddenly, computers weren't just for mathematicians, scientists, and *Star Trek* nerds—they were part of everyday life!

Think back to the first time you purchased something online—a book, a music download, a game, a pair of shoes, a hammer. Do you remember what you felt? Perhaps a surge of excitement tempered by an edge of trepidation? I can recall wondering whether consumers would purchase certain items—especially clothing—without seeing the merchandise in person and trying it on. Buying a pair of blue jeans online, for instance, seemed risky and might require the hassle of repacking and returning to the merchant.

This issue, of course, has proved significant but far from insurmountable.

It is but one of the many concerns you must anticipate and address with potential customers. Others include the ease with which they can find you, navigate your site or provider, locate products they desire, complete their purchase, complete their payment securely, and receive their goods. And while you can find numerous resources that address the technical details for each one of these, I encourage you to consider the overall experience.

Basically, the Golden Rule you once learned in Sunday school still provides insight as you think about your consumers and the shopping experience you want to provide to them. Jesus said, "Do to others what you would have them do to you" (Matt. 7:12), which compels us to put ourselves in someone else's shoes. This compassionate, respectful way of treating others holds up in all relationships, in this case the one with your prospective customer.

So I encourage you to go online, if you haven't already, and spend some time surfing and shopping for the same product or service you want to offer. This not only allows you to identify your competition, it also enables you to learn what you like and dislike about their respective shopping experiences. Which sites are easier to navigate than others? Which merchants engage your senses with graphics, photographs, music, and the brand's narrative voice? Which merchants use other e-commerce providers, such as eBay, Etsy, Amazon, or Alibaba, and which have their own independent dedicated websites?

As you've learned by now, being a good detective is crucial to being a great entrepreneur. It's not just doing research that improves the odds of getting your business off the ground and sustaining flight. It's how you integrate and assimilate the knowledge gleaned from your research and how you use it to influence your own designs that make the difference.

The Wright brothers didn't work in a vacuum and neither should you. They knew the history of past designs and flight attempts, from the "flying man" sketches of Leonardo da Vinci in the late fifteenth century to the gliders and hot air balloons tested by Sir George Caley and Otto Lilienthal. They studied and learned from the past mistakes and successes of their predecessors and contemporaries before they got off the ground at Kitty Hawk.

Whether you're building a physical business with an office and retail space or crafting virtual wings for the winds of cyberspace or both, you will benefit from once again emulating them.

Fly the Friendlier Skies

In the first decade of e-commerce, as it caught on and more and more people bought personal computers and purchased goods online, entrepreneurs wishing to penetrate this new market often hit a roadblock. Many felt they needed to know computer programming and online engineering in addition to business practices and economic expertise. As this new cyber landscape unfolded, it often felt like you had to be a pioneer willing to blaze new trails into uncharted territory.

Depending on your field of commerce and personal interest, this unfamiliarity and lack of expertise may have indeed been a major obstacle. You either had to invest considerable time in learning the intricacies of a field for which you may not have the interest or aptitude, or else you had to invest the money to pay computer engineers to create and maintain your online interface for you.

But that is no longer the case, my friend. Thanks to the Internet, you now have more opportunities to sell your products, goods, and services to the largest possible consumer base than ever before in history! The world has truly become a global marketplace where you can sit in your home in Seattle and conduct business with customers in Shanghai, Sydney, and Stockholm.

The aforementioned barriers have now been removed by the pioneers who have gone before you. You don't have to be a tech guru or computer genius to create your own website. Numerous businesses, both large and small as well as international and local, will assist you in creating and managing your site. A few of the dozens doing excellent, reputable work for e-commerce entrepreneurs include Jordan Crown (jordancrown.com), Followbright (followbright.com), and MaxAudience (maxaudience.com).

Search online and make contact with the ones that reflect quality, transparency, and excellent customer service. Check out customer comments and reviews, both on their site and around the Web and social media. Word gets out in a matter of seconds, so most reputable web designers have hundreds of positive reviews and satisfied customers to back their work.

Don't overlook your own backyard as well. Ask around for referrals from other business owners, friends, families, and coworkers. Despite the speed and convenience of online communication, it can sometimes be invaluable to meet face-to-face with an expert and have the person go over their services and answer your questions. Get several quotes, at least three, and be as specific as you can about what you want your website to provide—not just in looks but in the overall experience. Service providers will work within your budget and tell you what they can and cannot do in your price range.

You no longer have to venture into uncharted skies! Others have gone before you and mapped the air currents and altitude zones, allowing you to fly in friendlier skies. Always utilize as many resources as you can before investing time and money to discover what others already know.

Style and Error

Before you invest in creating your own website, however, I urge you to conduct some trial flights and test the winds of e-commerce. With the advantage of considerably more resources than those earlier trailblazers, you can choose a larger e-commerce platform to handle the logistics. Depending on what your product or service may be, you can choose one to use as your trial balloon.

For instance, let's say you've always loved taking beads, found objects, and old costume jewelry and creating new earrings, bracelets, and necklaces that express your unique aesthetic. While you've sold these casually to friends and family, you're now ready to get off the ground and fly beyond your familiar airport. You're torn between creating your own website and going with an e-commerce provider. The beauty of e-commerce at this time, however, is that you can do both!

You might decide to focus on the item that brings you the most compliments and the most sales among those who know you: earrings. From a production point of view, this item also requires less material and less of your precious time to produce a finished product. In other words, earrings would be the easiest jewelry item to make the most of in the least amount of time. So after making a dozen or two of these one-of-a-kind earrings, you set up shop on Etsy, an e-retailer known for hosting thousands of artisans, crafters, and designers and their creations.

If you are not familiar with Etsy or the provider you chose, obviously you need to become acquainted with its policies and procedures. Usually, these are outlined in the Q&A section or in the corporate "About" drop-down page. How will Etsy support your products? How will prospective customers browsing Etsy find your earrings? What key words best describe your style, materials, and vibe? On and on, you study and learn how the system works.

You can then jump-start your online business via Etsy by texting friends and family, announcing it on social media, or even sending emails. Soon you will begin receiving invaluable information based on how online consumers respond to your products. Do they want more photos with sharper details? More specific technical info about the materials used? A clearer sense of your personality and inspiration?

What about price point—any feedback either way? You want to maximize your profits without going over the imaginary tipping point where your target customer perceives your item as too costly for the value they would receive. If you've ever watched *Shark Tank*, you know that production costs and profit margins are some of the first questions investors ask. In addition to your materials and time invested, you will want to compare your prices with other, similar creations from competing artisans.

After you begin making sales and finding a rhythm, you will have a clearer idea who your actual customers really are—which is not necessarily always who you thought they would be. You might have been going for women between twenty-five and forty-five who work but discover that teen and young adult fashionistas between eighteen and thirty are your real market. Constantly plugged in to social media, your customers can often help you create a viral wind that turns into a sales storm.

Learning about your customers via e-commerce can also assist you in making in-person sales. Once you know who loves buying your jewelry, you likely can deduce more about her: the other places she shops, what she reads, where she works, the kind of home she lives in, her relational status, and so on. Armed over time with this information, you can seek out the accessories buyer for the upscale boutiques and funky jewelry stores where your customer shops. They might be interested in carrying a line of your products. If nothing else, they will now be aware of your creations and might be willing to spread the word.

Data about your customers will also help you determine how and when to expand your product offerings. After the earrings have hit your sales goal over several weeks or months, you add bracelets, responding to the requests from customers for this particular addition. Eventually, you may be able to add pendants, rings, and hair ornaments—but you will learn more if you begin slowly. If you try to make a vertical ascent, you may discover it impossible to sustain flight, even if you're able to reach 30,000 feet.

If you don't have physical products to offer, look for providers who connect customers with the services you offer. For instance, HomeAdvisor (homeadvisor.com) curates dozens of different home-related services and repairs, from house cleaning to architectural advice. If the first provider doesn't work or provide you with enough data for your next step, then try another.

Such experiments not only give you a sense of which way the wind is blowing, they also give you direct experience in the basics of e-commerce. There's no such thing as failing. You're learning by style and error! It's all about trying, learning, growing, observing, integrating, and knowing more than the last sale. The Internet provides a massive wind tunnel where you can test your e-commerce design without building and crashing your plane.

Mind Your Market

We cannot explore the endless entrepreneurial possibilities facilitated by e-commerce without discussing marketing and branding. Conceptually and practically, they must work hand in hand with your actual sales to reveal your public, corporate identity. You cannot separate one from the other without a ripple effect of consequences. Even if you decide not to engage in e-commerce, you must be familiar enough with it to know how to square off with your competitors that do.

You cannot ignore marketing and promoting your business online. I remember when big retailers like Sears and Penney's relied on catalog sales. Every Christmas this enormous volume of products would arrive in the mail, and my siblings and I would spend hours ogling the color photos of toys, games, and bikes in its pages, fighting over who would get what weeks later under the Christmas tree. Such reference books for childhood dreams not only promoted individual brands, such as Mattel and Hasbro, but served as the umbrella retailer over them all. While I'm sure direct-mail sales still exist, they have dwindled considerably and lost enormous market share to e-commerce.

When I was growing up, local retailers would often rely on mailing out flyers or postcards about their business, or they would advertise on local radio or television programs. And, of course, there was the indispensable Yellow Pages, listing line after line of categorized merchants, businesses, and services. While these all still exist in altered, e-compatible forms, their ability to drive customers to businesses has withered. When was the last time you actually retrieved your mail and stopped to browse through a catalog or to read the postcard from the new dry cleaner around the corner?

You must remember, though, that promoting, marketing, and advertising your business online guarantees absolutely nothing. If no one is finding your banners, reading your emails, or following you on social media, then it's no better than mailing them a flyer that's immediately thrown away. And this may be the most challenging, continually changing part of e-commerce: you have to know where and how to connect with your potential customers. You can invest and advertise with Facebook, but if you don't choose accurate filters to determine the recipients of your ad, your money is wasted.

This is why you must become a keen student and determined detective when it comes to discovering and leveraging points of contact with your target audience. When I first started combining various events into the epic family phenomenon known as MegaFest, I knew I needed corporate sponsors to underwrite the initial costs and supplement revenue brought in by tickets purchased in advance. I also knew that the right businesses and corporations could benefit tremendously from the sharply focused exposure they would receive from the several hundred thousand diverse individuals who would attend our multiday events and programming. With this win-win formula in mind, I drafted a wish list and had my team members begin making contact with businesses to gauge their interest in such a partnership.

Similarly, you must consider ways you can partner with other online retailers, bloggers, reviewers, and other websites related to your business. Ideally, you can come up with partnerships or collaborative endeavors that help you both achieve your goals. Obviously, some just want partners who will pay for sponsorship. But many others need your actual engagement. They need you to provide content for their blogs, interviews, product reviews, and industry analysis reports. Creating such content for them allows you to expand your expertise and your brand simultaneously.

And whether you realize it or not, you have already started branding your business.

Brand-New Day

We all know that it can be dangerous to judge a book by its cover. Similarly, the Internet has been exploited for numerous scams because it can be used to manipulate words and images and thereby to deceive others. Part of the Internet's initial allure was the way live communication could take place with a greater degree of control than in person. People could assume roles, project a scripted persona, or create avatars to shield their true identity, appearance, and personality. The same was true for online businesses as well.

Nonetheless, online usage and technology, particularly with social media, has brought transparency and authenticity to the forefront. Yes, people can fool you for a while, but the individuals and businesses whom clients and customers trust provide three key ingredients, which essentially comprises their brand: consistency, quality, and adaptability. Let's briefly consider each one.

Consistency means that your business name matches what you're actually selling and contributes to identifying your company's primary mission. Company names that are vague, generic, or bland tend to frustrate people who have no idea what your business goal actually is. Haven't we all seen commercials on TV or ads online that were cute, clever, or charming but never adequately spotlighted the company or product? Perhaps through enormous repetition, we might eventually come to associate the company with what we enjoy about the ad, but most businesses do not have this luxury.

Besides, just think about all the hundreds if not thousands of images, messages, sound bites, emails, texts, and tweets you receive on a daily basis, each clamoring for your undivided attention. As I recall reading, most research into marketing consistently reveals that a product or its promotional tool has only three seconds to engage potential consumers. Three seconds! But in that brief time, our brain has immediately started decoding the data our senses are feeding it, complete with visual imagery, sounds, smells, and texture.

Perhaps it's not that surprising if you think about how quickly you form a first impression of someone you've just met. Even if you don't realize you're analyzing your experience of them, your brain is processing how they look, the sound of their voice, the message they're saying, their scent, and the feel of their handshake. Your business may have even less time as you try to arrest the attention of individuals online.

Consistency in branding often goes a long way in communicating stability, security, and reliability. These qualities usually require frequency. When customers have the same experience with each purchase or interaction, they come to know what to expect from you and your business. As long as you repeatedly meet their positive expectations, your consistency provides fuel for your brand to grow.

Quality is an ingredient that remains self-evident in many cases.

Nevertheless, I'm often surprised by how many businesses do not attend to the details about the way they're branded, especially online. Released out into the world, anything tied to, associated with, or reflecting your business must reflect the attitude of excellence you want to maintain. Just as a sloppily dressed, unprepared interviewee doesn't get the job, if people find sloppy graphics, misspellings, and outdated information in your ad, blog entry, or website, they will likely pass you by.

Quality branding is all about paying close attention to details of functionality as well as sensory engagement. You want people to like and remember what they see online associated with you, your business, and your brand. Your brand must stand out and find a way to distinguish itself from your competition as well as from the cyber clutter we all face every day.

Adaptability, finally, is the complement to consistency. If your company's consistency ensures that your products and services always meet customers' satisfaction, you might be tempted to think that you should keep every aspect of your business the same. They like it now, so why change it, right? But as we've discussed, once you're airborne, you must still keep a close eye on winds and trends. As they often say about a pop culture phenomenon, one day you're in and the next day you're out.

Remaining flexible and adaptable allows you to change in order to keep meeting customers' positive expectations. No matter how good your product or customer service experience may be, you can't assume that today's means and methods will work tomorrow. You can always strive to be better and to experiment with improvements. Technology is always changing and you don't want to get locked in to an outdated mode of e-commerce. Social and cultural winds also change the retail landscape, and you want to maximize their power to fly higher with your brand.

Blue Sky for Every Business

As we conclude our brief foray into e-commerce, I hope this chapter has given you food for thought and fuel for your journey through the cyber clouds. To recap, if you don't remember anything else I've shared in this chapter, here's what I hope you remember about e-commerce. First, you can't ignore it because it's not going away. It's almost been a quarter century since entrepreneurs began to fly into this new, untested airspace. Since then, many have soared and continue to climb while others have crashed only to fly again another day. Overall, though, e-commerce continues to reveal plenty of blue sky for every business.

Second, e-commerce presents unlimited opportunities for test-marketing and experimentation, which helps you learn more about what works and who your customers are. You have this classroom, laboratory, and wind tunnel all in one where you can explore and get your bearings before embarking on a longer, more extensive journey.

Finally, e-commerce is absolutely essential for success in promoting, marketing, and branding your business, whether you actually attempt to sell online or not. No serious, profitable entrepreneur can afford to ignore the vast reach and influential impact that the Internet has had on every business model in existence.

Remember, the *e* in e-commerce stands for easy!

PART III

CLEAR THE CLOUDS

Who are these that fly like a cloud, and like doves to their windows?

—Isaiah 60:8 ESV

CHAPTER 7

Flight Crew

Assembling Your Dream Team

*Coming together is a beginning. Keeping together is progress.
Working together is success.*

—Henry Ford

Early in my career as an entrepreneur, I faced one of the battles no one ever wants to fight, let alone someone trying to keep a business airborne. A contractor I had used for a new project filed a frivolous lawsuit against my company in hope of cashing in on my rapidly accelerating ascent as both a businessman and pastor.

I suspect this adversary believed I would settle quietly, despite having done nothing wrong, in order to avoid the inevitable publicity that comes from criminal accusations, no matter how unsubstantiated they may be. But they didn't know who they were dealing with! I was not about to let my budding enterprise be hijacked by someone attempting to eject me from the cockpit.

As the court date approached, I prepared for the skirmish armed with my own attorneys and personal knowledge of the situation. I had already prayed for the peace that passeth understanding so that

I wouldn't strangle anyone making false accusations in the court-room! So I mentally and spiritually defended myself, clinging to the honesty and integrity I had worked so hard to establish in my business dealings as well as my ministry. Anticipating something out of a John Grisham novel, or at least an old episode of *Perry Mason*, I was surprised that, when the court hearing occurred, it was actually anticlimactic.

An even bigger surprise was my impression of the lawyer representing my opponent, the plaintiff in this suit the contractor had filed. The opposing counsel wasn't impressive because of his eloquence or any glamorous, star qualities in his performance. His appearance was professional but not flashy. In fact, there was nothing slick about this gentleman—he simply knew the law and had a clear strategy for presenting his client's case. He obviously had anticipated all questions thrown at his client and was prepared with the right answers.

Weeks later, after the matter had been resolved and the dust settled, I called this attorney, complimented his courtroom demeanor, and asked him to lunch. Surprised to hear from me, he nonetheless agreed to meet, and over lunch we got better acquainted. Finally, I shared with him my observations about his professional abilities in the courtroom and revealed why I had asked to meet with him: to offer him a job!

Shocked that I would make such an offer, he asked several astute follow-up questions before requesting time to think about it, pray about it, as well as discuss it with his wife and family. The next day I was delighted when he called and accepted my offer, and he began working for me two weeks later. This gentleman went on to represent all of my businesses for more than a decade, proving my judgment about him accurate as he exceeded my expectations time and time again. Despite being on opposite sides in that initial legal proceeding, we went on to work together successfully in numerous entrepreneurial endeavors.

You're Hired

Now it may appear that I hired this man rather impulsively, but nothing could be further from the truth. Yes, my initial impression of him triggered my interest in his abilities and how he might fit into my organization. But during the interval between when our case ended and when I asked him to lunch that day, I had done my due diligence. I had researched his background, his educational training, and his professional reputation among his peers as well as his clients. Every piece of research confirmed my hunch that he would be an asset for TDJ Enterprises.

There was still risk involved, of course, because there is risk with any new hire no matter how well you think you know the person. But I had done everything in my power to maximize the likelihood of this man's success as my employee. While it was tempting to dismiss the possibility of hiring him because of his adversarial role in the context of our first meeting, allowing that context to block my hiring him would have been a mistake. Indeed, seeing him operate in such a situation told me volumes more about his character and credentials than any interview could have ever provided.

Sometimes our adversaries can become some of our greatest allies. Keep in mind that you don't have to like someone or want to be friends with them in order to hire them. If they're good at their job and share the same dedication to excellence that you have, it doesn't matter if you like the same sports teams or share similar backgrounds. You don't have to have them over for Sunday dinner, but you do have to be able to rely on them to fulfill the responsibilities for which you hired them.

Hiring friends (and family—but more about relatives in a moment) is often dangerous and can kill your business faster than lightning hitting your plane's engine. When you hire a friend, you automatically make it harder on yourself to push this person to their best performance. In theory, you might think it's easier because of the rapport you have already established. You already know each other and know how to communicate, right?

But here's the problem: usually you want your friends to keep on being your friends, and so ultimately the friendship gets in the way of the entrepreneurship. You let things slide because you don't want to risk hurting their feelings or stepping on their toes. You don't hold them accountable to the same standard as an employee who's not a friend, and as a result your business suffers.

Generally in business it's better if you separate your personal relationships from your professional ones, but I'm convinced it's absolutely crucial for entrepreneurs. You're hiring someone for their abilities, talents, and the overall value they bring to your company— not their favorite jokes and family recipes. When you want your car fixed, you don't care whether the mechanic is friendly or not—you just want someone who knows how to solve your problem at a fair price. The same goes for finding a doctor. You might like her and you might not, but what matters is how knowledgeable and skilled she is at treating your particular ailment or condition.

If you like an employee and end up being friends without it affecting their performance, then count yourself blessed and enjoy this rare feat. But most of the time, your business will benefit and grow more quickly if you keep communications clear and boundaries firm. Hire the best person for the role you need filled and to do the job you need done as effectively as possible. Do the due diligence required to see if their past performance, job history, and education equip them for your company's needs. Again, this does not guarantee that they will be as strong as you expect, but it increases the odds.

And if the person doesn't work out after adequate training and multiple opportunities to improve, then don't waste time—yours or theirs. The old adage "slow to hire and quick to fire" holds up in my experience. So take your time to find the best people in whom you can invest as leaders within your business. Get to know them professionally and if at all possible see them in action doing what you need them to do.

Many entrepreneurs hire people because they have a sudden need due to unexpected growth or increased business. As a result, they hire someone who is immediately available instead of using temps or finding other solutions for their short-term need. This kind of hiring rarely produces a quality employee who grows with the company over the long haul. So you end up having to fire those hires and start over again, which may not seem like a big deal, but it surely can be when your business is small and just starting out.

When you're building something from scratch, those first few hires are crucial if you are to continue flying successfully. You want team members who not only understand your products, services, and customers, but ones who also grasp your vision for success. They don't have to know how you built your plane or how to fly it, but they do need to know how their contribution affects the rest of your passengers.

Cast Your Net

My mother used to say, "If you see a turtle sitting on a fence post, you can always know he didn't get there by himself!" She was right!

And if you see an entrepreneur interviewed about the success of his or her business, then you can be certain that many others contributed to their journey.

You can't do mighty deeds by yourself in isolation. If you have a vision to build a venture that will fly and sustain its journey through the clouds, you will not be able to do it alone. Drawing on your existing network of relationships as well as cultivating the new and necessary relationships you need ensures you have the flight crew you need to soar.

While it may be tempting to be a Superman or Wonder Woman and try to launch your business by yourself, it doesn't take long to realize the limitations of your superpowers. In fact, people who see themselves as the be-all and end-all in their spheres of influence nose-dive and crash a long way from their potential. They view themselves as solo pilots but forget that even Charles Lindbergh only made one solo transatlantic flight! Never forget that defying gravity and reaching your destination is a journey you cannot make alone.

If you try to do everything your business requires, then you're guaranteed to crash and burn. Real superpowers require a variety of complementary talents and abilities working in harmony to achieve results beyond what you could achieve by sheer talent or hard work alone. As one person, you are limited by a finite amount of time, energy, and ability. You have only two hands and can only accomplish what two hands are capable of accomplishing. You must assemble the best team possible to support, sustain, and soar with your new venture.

I like to remind the business leaders I'm privileged to coach never to forget the "net" in networking. Nets are woven strands of roped fibers designed to contain certain items while letting others pass through. Nets provide a flexible filter to help anglers, athletes, and entomologists snare their fish, field goals, and fireflies!

Similarly, our business networks are most effective when we extend our interests and engage with entrepreneurs, consumers, and other business leaders going in directions different than our own. I'm convinced the most dynamic, resourceful networks are built on strands of connectivity that cross barriers and integrate diverse perspectives. They increase the size and depth of the pool from which you can draw supporters, investors, employees, and customers.

Ground Crew

Everyone needs encouragement and support, especially as they embark on a new voyage of personal and professional discovery. Ideally, every new entrepreneur would enjoy the benefit of three different kinds of ground crew members: supporters, advisers, and mentors. These relationships are not essential to your endeavor's success but they usually lay the groundwork for the smooth runway you need in order to take flight. While these roles may overlap, let's consider each of these encouragers and the unique contributions they make to your overall achievement.

Supporters tend to be the people you consider your greatest fans, the ones who celebrate your triumphs with you as well as pick up the pieces when you fall. For many entrepreneurs, their families provide this kind of support and personal care. Family members not only encourage your endeavors and serve as a sounding board, they also provide practical support in the form of picking up your kids from school, cooking a meal from time to time, or offering to help out with household chores.

More than just cheerleaders, supporters understand the cost required for you to be fully invested in your new business, and they care about you and will do what they can to help you succeed. They believe in you even if they don't understand what your business is about or why you feel compelled to launch it. They provide personal, emotional support through the grueling process of starting your business.

Advisers, on the other hand, give you professional, intellectual support, usually in the form of their counsel and wisdom. They may care about you personally but have more to offer you in the form of their best business practices. They are often entrepreneurs themselves and have already experienced many of the initial challenges you are facing. They want to help you avoid the same mistakes they made so that you can make your business more successful.

Their advice may be specific and practical: you should order supplies from this wholesaler and not that one; or it may be more general and conceptual: always take one day off each week no matter how busy you are. The most effective advisers usually have some knowledge or experience with your kind of product, service, and customer base. They know firsthand how to sell cakes or start a dry cleaner because they've done it before.

Mentors combine both of these roles, the supporter and the adviser, and offer comprehensive insight into how to juggle your life's demands as an entrepreneur with those of being a spouse, parent, caregiver, or student. They want you to succeed professionally but not at the expense of your personal life and family coherence. They know that in order to truly succeed you must never lose sight of life balance and the priority of loving those most important in your life.

Of these three supporting roles, mentors are typically the most difficult to find and to sustain. It can also be difficult to define your expectations and have another busy, successful individual agree to commit to mentoring you. Don't presume that the person is always going to be older than you or a grizzled veteran nearing retirement age. While mentors are often wiser and more experienced than you, this may or may not correspond with their chronological age. They may have started working in your field at a young age while you are only now switching careers, or they may have come from a family that owned a business in your industry.

No matter what you call them, these people in supporting roles, what I like to think of as your ground crew, help prepare you for flight and refuel you in between your journeys. They are essential to your success, so never underestimate their importance. Don't be afraid to ask for what you need in order to succeed!

Flight Crew

In addition to your ground crew, you will need people willing to invest more than just emotional support, personal encouragement, and inspiring advice. You need a flight crew to fund your new venture and get it off the ground. And this team must begin with you as the captain piloting the process. You must be willing to invest your own financial resources into your business if you expect others to risk theirs. So before you print copies of your business plan and rehearse your pitch for banks, backers, and venture capitalists, you should have already lined up your own investment.

Deciding how much you can invest in your new business is tricky. If you can't afford to lose your investment, then you need to wait until you have saved enough to properly stake your business. Many entrepreneurs, fueled by the adrenaline thrill and excitement of starting their new venture, recklessly deplete all their savings, their retirement fund, and their home equity.

While I admire such dedication and willingness to go "all in," I must caution you not to allow your passion to override practicality. I have never gambled on games of chance, but others who apparently enjoy such activities tell me they consider their wagers recreational. The key, so they tell me, is never to bet more than you can afford to lose.

The same holds true for entrepreneurs betting on their new business. Risk is a necessity, but you must also consider worst-case scenarios. Don't invest all you have in something that hasn't yet proved it can fly. Only invest what you can reasonably afford, making sure you have a contingency plan for how you will survive and pay your bills if the business fails before it becomes profitable. The best entrepreneurs assume it will take several attempts, including several infusions of capital, before their business takes flight and remains airborne, and they plan accordingly.

So be smart about what you can invest. Write down your assets and liabilities and see what makes sense. Discuss what you want to invest with your spouse or others directly affected by your investment. Consult your accountant to provide objective perspective as well as to help you think through the various tax implications.

Once you've determined what your investment will be, then you can more confidently pitch others who may be interested in funding your business. If you've ever watched *Shark Tank*, you know this is often the first question the panel of professional investors asks the would-be entrepreneur making a pitch. They want to know how much skin this person has in the game in order to gauge the individual's level of commitment and threshold for risk.

Depending on the amount of capital you need, one investor may be enough to stake your venture. More than likely, however, you will need several key investors to fuel your flight. These investors are often successful business owners and experienced entrepreneurs already. They hear many pitches from the full spectrum of would-be entrepreneurs looking for cash, and as a result, these investors say no much more frequently than yes.

So be prepared to be turned down a few times and use the experience to improve your pitch. Respectfully ask all declining investors why they're unwilling to invest in your venture at this time. Some may not be willing to comment, but others will provide you with honest feedback about their concerns.

Listen carefully to their words and the reasoning behind their decision to decline. If they have doubts about your location, ask them for suggestions about where to relocate. If they struggle to understand the product or service you're selling, then sharpen and clarify your pitch. Use the opportunity to turn that investor's no into the next investor's yes!

Get It in Writing

When you finally find investors willing to back your venture, then you must discuss the details of how their investment will be repaid and their specific share of your profits. While handshakes are good, you should both require a written contract spelling out the particulars of your agreement. If you aren't clear on the exact commitment such a contract requires of you, then consult an attorney, financial expert, or accountant to review the document and explain it to you. Never sign something you haven't read! No matter how much you trust the other party, mistakes get made and misunderstandings occur.

Finally, make sure you and your investors discuss the extent of their role beyond providing funds. Will they have any authority to make decisions or influence directions for your business? Do you need to have their approval before making major decisions? There's a big difference between an investor, who is usually just risking capital in hope of profiting from your future success, and a partner, director, or stakeholder.

People who want a role in your business and a chance to fly the plane every now and then can be huge assets. If they believe in you, share your vision, and have the skill set and availability to participate beyond merely investing, they become your copilots. They not only have a stake in your profits, they also participate on a daily basis to shape the company and run operations.

With such stakeholders, it is even more imperative to determine their role and job responsibilities before the business is off the ground. Clarify each other's expectations and delegate the specific areas of responsibility within the venture. Establish trust with open, honest communication that respects one another and values collaborative efforts. Decide how conflicts will be handled and final decisions made before the heat of the moment when new orders are coming in and directions have to be chosen.

Collaborations can be challenging for new entrepreneurs used to being a solo act. They may not initially appreciate having someone else question, challenge, or overturn their decisions. But being overly possessive of your "baby" may deprive you of precious opportunities for dynamic new directions. So make sure you work only with partners whom you respect and are willing to listen to. Nothing is worse than having a shareholder in your business play backseat driver when you're in the pilot's seat.

On the other hand, allowing stakeholders to participate in the process of your business provides a richer, more multifaceted perspective. You also have others to share the workload and provide you with support when you stumble. The Bible says, "Two are better than one, because they have a good return for their labor" and "A cord of three strands is not quickly broken" (Ecc. 4:9; 4:12). So put your ego aside if necessary and enjoy the opportunity to launch your business with others as invested in its success as you are.

All in the Family

Aside from banks, professional investors, and venture capitalists, many new entrepreneurs turn to family and friends for funding. While it's natural to assume those who know and love you the most would want to invest in your new venture, the reality is often more complicated and challenging. First and foremost, there is absolutely no way for you or those closest to you to remain objective about the investment.

Try as you may, it's difficult to separate family dynamics from business practices. Aunt Ruth and Uncle Boaz may know that you're an adult with a degree and ten years' experience as a chef, but when they invest in your catering business, they still see you as their little niece selling Girl Scout cookies.

Don't get caught in the trap of past perceptions. Discuss the specifics with relatives just as you would with any investor you just met. Set clear boundaries and establish realistic expectations. Discuss what happens if the business fails and they lose their investment. How will they handle such a loss and how might that change the dynamic of your relationship? Don't wait until no one will pass the turkey to you at Thanksgiving to realize they have a problem with you!

Always have a contract, but when family or close friends invest in your business, it's even more essential. It may feel awkward or uncomfortable at first, but if both of you seriously want to make the relationship work, then you must write out the details. Don't just smile and hug and act like everything's okay and assume because they're family they would never withdraw their investment or even enter into litigation! We've all heard of dozens of situations where once-close siblings, or even parents and adult children, no longer speak to one another because of the emotions wrapped around a failed family business.

Equally essential is determining the role these familiar investors will have in your business. Will they have access to all your operations, practices, and records? Do they have a voice in the decisions? Because whether they have one on paper or not, most family members automatically consider themselves stakeholders. If you welcome their input or can at least tolerate it, then there will be no surprises down the line. But if you've always thought your mother-in-law was up in your business before, just wait until she's invested in your new venture!

Who's the Boss?

While we're discussing family as investors, we should also consider the complications that arise when you employ family members. The problem is that you will expect more from them while they may assume they can give less. Because you're related, share past history, or have a close relationship, you may assume that they will give 110 percent just like you will be giving. These loved ones, however, may expect to collect a salary without having to work as hard as they might for a boss they don't know in any other role.

Personally, I have employed family members in a number of ventures with mostly positive results. I've tried to make my expectations clear to them up front and asked them outright if they can contribute what the business needs. Depending on their talents and experience, I've done my best to challenge them without burdening them. As I would with any employee, I want them to grow and stretch their abilities and become more proficient at making the business successful.

I've also separated their role as my employee from our relationship as parent and child or whatever the connection might be. When we're working and focusing on business, then we're not discussing their cousin's new car or who was voted off their favorite reality show the night before. And when we're having a family dinner, event, or holiday, then we're not going to talk shop.

When hiring family members, make it clear beforehand that their job responsibilities will likely change over time and that their position may be eliminated, depending on the pace of sales, economic climate, and other business variables. Ask them not to go behind your back and discuss problems at work with other family members outside the business, which means of course that you commit to doing the same. Try to remind each other that your relationship comes before your roles so that if it's clear one has to change, you both know ahead of time that it will be the role.

I would caution you to think carefully before hiring a family member and to make sure the potential benefits are worth the risk. Never pull in a family member just for a short-term solution to your staffing needs—that's what temp agencies are for. Once again, you're setting yourself up to be disappointed and potentially damaging your relationship over something that's not worth it.

When it works well and the business thrives, there's nothing better than sharing your joy, as well as your profits, with family. The flipside, though, is just as true. There's no greater threat to killing your passion, purpose, and profits than when the business comes between loved ones. So don't risk losing the very people you love and are motivated to share your success with if you, or they, have reservations.

What They Really Want

The relationships you establish with your clients and customers will ultimately determine whether your business soars. They are the lifeblood of your business and can dramatically influence its over-all health and profitability. And you must realize that you are sell-ing and providing much more than just your product or service. As we've already discussed, you are solving a problem for your cus-tomer. You're selling them a solution, plain and simple.

In many cases, you're not only solving their problem but you're also providing something intangible they want or need. I recall shopping in a high-end men's clothing store in New York once. The manager, who turned out to also be the owner, was absolutely perfect in assisting customers. He was attentive without hovering, helpful without being pushy, honest in his opinions regardless of how they might tilt a potential purchase. Whether waiting on a con-struction worker in dirty coveralls, a Wall Street banker, or a soc-cer mom shopping for her teenaged son, the owner treated everyone with courtesy, respect, and genuine interest.

After browsing and observing him in action, I complimented him on his attitude and demeanor and asked about the secret to his suc-cess. He smiled and said, "With every customer, I ask myself what I can do to make sure they have a pleasant experience that will make them want to come back. Even if they don't buy something today, how can I influence them to return when they need to purchase something here in the future? Obviously, it's not the same for every customer so the real key is *listening* to and *engaging* with what each customer tells you they need."

This gentleman was absolutely right. In his business, some cus-tomers come in and buy a suit, but what they're really buying is confidence for that job interview that's coming up. The older busi-nessman browsing new cuff links and ties is actually looking for a way to show he's made it. The woman shopping for socks and under-wear for her husband isn't there to buy socks and underwear—she's there to show her man how special he is, how much she recognizes and appreciates his uniqueness. If she just wanted socks and under-wear for him, she could go to any department store at the mall!

The manager at this men's store realized the psychology of his particular clientele. He understood that not only is quality merchandise important for the people willing to pay more for men's clothing and accessories, but the atmosphere and experience must also be compelling. Everyone longs to be treated like a person of value and respected as a fellow human being. We've all been in shops, stores, or restaurants where we felt mistreated or neglected. And most of us have not returned!

If you listen to your customers and engage with what they really want from your business, then you will grow. You don't have to make a change based on every customer suggestion, but you should consider it. Even if what a customer requests is too expensive, too unrealistic, or too impossible, listen to the message below their request. What's behind their request or suggestion? What are they really wanting? More value for their money, lower prices, better service, a more convenient location, or longer store hours? Some customers merely want to be heard, to be recognized as having an opinion.

Race to the Top

The final relationship you must cultivate is with your competition. Many entrepreneurs overlook this crucial relationship, erroneously assuming that because they're competing for the same customers they should avoid any kind of interaction. As the old saying goes, "Keep your friends close and your enemies closer."

While competitors aren't your enemies, they are still important to know and to watch closely. In many ways, having competition forces you to bring your A game and hold nothing back. Seeing the way others market, promote, and sell their products and services can often inspire you as well. Coke and Pepsi need each other to stretch and strive to exceed the other in sales. Similarly with McDonald's and Burger King, Walmart and Target, Apple and Samsung.

I don't recommend simply imitating what your competitors are doing, but learning from their methods and mistakes can often save you valuable time and money. Knowing what customers like about their customer service, shipping, or returns can help you adjust and improve your own systems. When you know your competition, then you can also be more specific about what sets you apart from them. You can attempt to offer a distinctive approach, proprietary product, or unique service that other, similar businesses do not.

If you approach other, similar entrepreneurs with courtesy and respect instead of hostility and envy, you might be surprised how you can help each other. Every business needs to be able to refer customers to a similar one at times when they have reached capacity and cannot serve their customers. I'm always especially grateful when a restaurant or hotel provides me with another comparable suggestion when they cannot book my reservation for the date and time needed.

It might seem like a strange kind of customer service, but it truly works in your favor because you're still being helpful to a potential customer. If you can't serve them with your business, then you can at least help them with your attitude and information. You might recall in the classic movie *Miracle on 34th Street* the way Santa Claus, employed by Macy's during the holiday season, refers busy moms to other stores to find the best deals on toys. At first, Santa is fired for losing potential customers, but then the unselfish attitude and goodwill generated by his referrals prove to be a brilliant promotional move. Hundreds of new customers flock to the store, eager to support a store seemingly more committed to the Christmas spirit than to profit.

Building solid relationships with your competitors and other entrepreneurs can also help you when it's time to expand, adjust, or sell your business. How many mergers have taken place between rival companies that joined forces to become a giant in their industry? Depending on changes and advancements with your product or service, you may also discover that the playing field expands so rapidly that there is more than enough room for numerous competitors.

Just look at the number of cell phone carriers going head-to-head these days. When mobile phone technology was new, only a couple of companies handled most consumers. But as the technology becomes less expensive and more accessible, there's room for more companies to target the millions of users in any given area, region, or country. And as a result, service has generally gotten better for all customers.

Competitors can also help you expand your network and extend your reach into new neighborhoods and communities, building relationships that can support and sustain your business long after you're airborne. And if you want to soar, your entrepreneurial relationships must extend beyond your customers, employees, coworkers, and competitors.

In order to reach new heights, you will need to cultivate relationships from a wide spectrum of professional and personal endeavors. If you network only with people who do what you do, buy what you sell, and have what you have, then there's no opportunity for your chemistry to ignite and catalyze in new, creative ways. You might sell your new and improved mop or wig, but you won't have the flight crew needed to land, refuel, and continue to your ultimate destination of success.

I've been inspired in my business practices by seeing native women in Nairobi weaving baskets, Australian Aborigines carving boomerangs, and sidewalk vendors in Times Square hawking knockoffs. I've also been blessed to encounter a wide and diverse population of creative thinkers, artists, leaders, ministers, inventors, and innovators. At first glance, their field of study or line of work may seem to have nothing to do with my endeavors. But once we begin talking and comparing notes, my mind begins turning in new directions and looking for transferable traits and mirrored methods. Remaining open to a wide body of relationships enables me to replenish my creativity and to hone my problem-solving skills.

If you want to be a successful entrepreneur, you are who you know!

CHAPTER 8

What Goes Up Must Come Down

Entrepreneurial Leadership 101

Start with the end in mind.
—Stephen R. Covey

In the aftermath of the devastation that we have come to know as 9/11, a persistent rumor circulated about the flight training the terrorists received here in our country. Apparently, a number of them had enrolled at flight schools in the United States as part of their undercover subterfuge. Shortly after they transformed four airliners into weapons of mass destruction on that fateful day in September, reports emerged that the terrorists had requested lessons on flying planes but not on landing them. Because they knew how their horrific hijacking would end, there was no need to understand the logistics involved in landing the jumbo jetliners they planned to commandeer.

While this allegation has never been indisputably verified, it nonetheless emphasizes an essential point in our flight training as entrepreneurs: the importance of knowing how to land your plane before you take off. This ability to see the big picture and control the process as much as possible is fundamental to being an entrepreneurial leader. It's what separates the ultrasuccessful from those who simply reach a certain altitude and coast on autopilot.

You see, it's not enough just to get your new venture off the ground—you must determine where, when, and how you want to return this flying machine to earth. Even if it changes its flight path along the way, you need to know what to do with what you build. Otherwise, you're doomed to crash into whatever obstacles arise to block your path to success.

Begin at the End

You may be surprised to be told to consider the evolution of your enterprise while it's still in its infancy, but you must extend your vision to include the mature result you hope from the beginning to fulfill. Thinking through the conclusion of this epic story you are writing may seem impossible at this point because so many variables of your success are yet to be determined. And while it's true you will encounter many ups and downs that must be evaluated and integrated throughout your flight, you nonetheless must do everything in your power to prepare for the future landing you hope to secure.

Is this new business one you hope to pass on to your children and grandchildren or to sell and liquidate after ten years? Are you hoping to be bought out by a large conglomerate competitor or are you dreaming of taking your private venture public by selling shares to global investors? Are you motivated to launch this side-hustle to supplement your retirement income or are you wanting something to engage your imagination and profit from the years of experience you had working for someone else? Do you want a passive partnership that will guarantee retirement income or would you rather have a lump sum right now?

Knowing what you hope, envision, want, and would like to happen is crucial to how you build your vision from the ground up. With a sense of your ideal future landing strip in mind, you can make many other choices with much more accuracy, efficiency, and intentionality. In fact, beginning with the end in mind will make many of your daily decisions for you.

For example, from my dealings in real estate, I've learned many investors will buy a property knowing they intend to flip it—to renovate, remodel, and redesign it before reselling it for a profit. These investors usually ignore their own personal tastes and style preferences in favor of more generic, neutral colors and décor. They want their investment property to appeal to the broadest consumer market possible.

They also choose more modestly priced materials to keep costs down. Sometimes they can even buy fixtures, finishes, and furniture for a lower cost in bulk to use for several properties, not just one. Because they know their goal and their time line, they don't spend over budget on high-end, distinctive design elements that would appeal only to a handful of buyers. Instead, they're planning their venture to land in a way that will allow them to exit with the maximum profit from their investment.

Another benefit of anticipating potential problems before they develop is that you then have a procedural solution in place should they arise. When setting up contracts with the many vendors and subcontractors my companies sometimes use, I make sure that we include a clear arbitration clause in case something goes off track. We include these rules of disengagement while everyone is friendly and enthused about our collaboration because we know that it can become very challenging to communicate when conflicts occur and we're at odds.

It's the same reason why many couples sign prenuptial agreements before they walk down the aisle and tie the knot of matrimony. They know it's easier to come up with practical rules of dissolving their union while they still have stars in their eyes instead of waiting until the aliens of anger, jealousy, and infidelity crash-land onto their once-perfect planet.

With your venture, consider how you would ideally want to leave the business. If your name is on the business or closely associated with it, are you willing to allow your name to be used after you sell? What about your image? Many successful ventures sell their name or buy the rights to partner with another company so that their names and brands become associated.

This often happens in the world of professional sports. Not long ago, I was excited to have an opportunity to talk to Randall Stephenson, the chairman and CEO of AT&T, and listen as he shared morsels of wisdom that I was eager to glean. As the conversation ebbed and flowed, he mentioned the "naming rights" he had acquired from another Dallas-based business icon, the renowned Jerry Jones, for the stadium Jerry built as a home for the Cowboys. The building remains the same but the corporate name brings brand awareness for AT&T and strengthens the stadium's influence as well.

Thinking through how you will handle such issues as naming rights, marketing slogans, and proprietary products when you launch your venture can save considerable time, energy, and money down the road should opportunities or conflicts arise. In many cases, anticipating what could go wrong before it happens allows you to prevent some of those conflicts from ever arising. If you know you struggle with being organized and keeping good records, then make sure you hire professionals to assist you in these areas of personal weakness. If you have a gift for inventing new product lines but struggle to market them, find ways to compensate for and alleviate this challenge.

No matter what your dream entails, if you want it to ascend and reach new heights, you must consider how it will eventually come down. Seeing the entire arc of your venture's trajectory enables you to maximize the opportunities for success that may arise along the way. Otherwise, all your effort may only set you up for a terrible crash.

Just because you can fly doesn't mean you're ready to soar!

Patents Require Patience

The Wright brothers knew this essential truth of entrepreneurial leadership. Once they got their plane off the ground, they kept refining their winged flyer by stabilizing its pitch, improving control, and testing maneuverability. In fact, when the Wright brothers finally launched their flying machine at Kitty Hawk, they didn't respond the way you might expect—there were no press conferences, major headlines, or public celebrations. Instead they demonstrated the kind of leadership, intelligence, strategy, and timing every entrepreneur needs. They kept their ultimate goal in mind—not just to fly but to maximize their invention's full potential.

They knew their flyer wasn't ready to soar just yet, so after their initial success in 1903 Orville and Wilbur returned to their family's home in Dayton, Ohio, and began testing new versions of their airplane in a remote cow pasture known as Huffman Prairie. Without the strong wind currents of the Carolina coast to power their plane, these resourceful brothers built a giant catapult to create the same effect. While they knew they could have sold tickets and put on record-breaking exhibitions, they instead chose to work in relative obscurity because they didn't want others copying their designs.

Even after they worked out the bugs and arrived at a consistent, practical model in 1905, the Wrights took their plane apart, crated it, and stored it—for more than two years! They wanted to secure the patent for their flying machine, which in turn would allow them to sell their invention. While waiting on their patent, they began to discreetly test the waters for potential buyers of this new technology.

By the time their patent was granted in 1906, the Wright brothers, envisioning their invention's many possibilities for military usage, arranged demonstrations for the US and French governments. Negotiations were particularly tricky because the brothers refused to demonstrate their planes without contracts in place. The two governments, of course, refused to offer contracts without seeing what they were buying. What could have been a deal-breaking stalemate turned into an opportunity to build trust. Both sides compromised with contracts in place that would not be finalized until after officials witnessed the new flying machine themselves.

After mutually agreed upon negotiations, Orville went to Arlington, Virginia, while his older brother, Wilbur, sailed overseas to perform in Le Mans, France. It was the first time they had separated since beginning the pursuit of their dream, but it was necessary since each would need to pilot their invention before these two vitally important audiences. Circumstances and weather patterns worked against them in both demonstrations, but eventually they proved themselves and the whole world took notice. Suddenly, two quiet, unknown bicycle-shop owners from Dayton, Ohio, were the first international celebrities of the twentieth century.

Flying Low

The Wright brothers' process has much to teach us about how to begin with the end in mind. Alongside their intense passion for inventing a flying machine was a shrewd business sensibility. They knew that certain parts of the process must precede others, and they patiently followed a synchronized schedule.

Today, when someone starts a new company or invents a new device, the person immediately tweets it, posts it, and calls a press conference. Twenty-first-century entrepreneurs know they need to get the word out and capture the attention of their prospective customers for their business to get off the ground. In our 24/7 online-all-the-time world, they have to seize every opportunity to get their message out as frequently as possible if they expect to have any shot at penetrating the market and capturing public attention.

But I advise you to consider the timing of your launch announcements. You don't want to start a viral wildfire that may burn out before your business can successfully feed its flames. Many new entrepreneurs fail because they focus on promoting and marketing their new venture more than on testing and improving the business itself.

Like someone who thinks they're in love because they're infatuated with the idea of being in love, these individuals aren't nearly as passionate about their product or service as they are about simply being an entrepreneur! They assume that getting their name in front of everyone makes them a successful leader.

Often driven by their egos, these types are all sizzle and no bacon, and it doesn't take customers long to figure this out. These would-be pilots inadvertently and prematurely crash their opportunities to soar because they don't take the time to ensure their engines can travel at the requisite speeds for higher altitudes. Good pilots know how to warm up their plane's engines and then stabilize flight at lower altitudes before climbing higher. They know when it's time to consider landing and to find an open runway.

The best entrepreneurs initially focus on their product and its process more than its promotion. They do test-marketing and enlist the help of focus groups, paying close attention to the responses they receive. Then they explore their networks, looking for key individuals to advise them on which changes to make and how. They know not to take every critique to heart, and instead they find a way to integrate customer feedback while maintaining the integrity of their unique product or service. They view setbacks as opportunities to improve and to recalibrate the coordinates for their destination.

Sometimes those lessons learned early in the launching of your venture may become elusive as you grow with your success. My friend Tyler Perry knows this firsthand and told me that he had recently toured with a new play because he wanted to experience the audience's honest response to new characters, story lines, and dialogue.

Taking the show on the road gave him a chance to check the pulse of his audience by being connected with them in the way achieved only by live performances. It was like having a huge focus group every night!

So remember, nothing you do in the process of pursuing your entrepreneurial destination will be wasted. You may not see how some of your early mistakes and missteps can help you, but they are essential for your ultimate success. Learning while you lead determines the kind of leader you will become.

The Thrill of the Kill

I was recently talking to a group of new entrepreneurs, all of them from the millennial generation. I'm always intrigued to hear from the next generation of innovators, artists, and inventors, and this group was no exception. As we continued to converse, I sensed their frustration with the slow process of profitability and with their overall lack of vision for where they eventually wanted to land with their new ventures. They knew they wanted to succeed, but their vision from the cockpit was still blurry.

When they began describing various stalled or stillborn projects, I sensed them internally questioning the directions their passions were taking them and contemplating exit strategies in search of other career options. In other words, they were considering landing their planes when they had barely gotten off the ground!

So I asked them, "What is it that you're really wanting right now? Do you really want to quit doing what you know you love? What could these various setbacks be telling you about what you need to do next?"

One young woman, a talented vocalist and producer, paused thoughtfully and then said, "You know what I really want? I want to be respected and taken seriously. I want to call up other artists and have them listen to my creative vision for their next album or EP. I want other producers and media execs to give me a chance."

The rest of the group nodded encouragingly as a brilliant tech gamer added, "It's like when I was a boy and wanted to be seen and taken seriously as a man. I wanted to move from the fringes where the kids were and come and sit with the grown-ups around the fire."

I loved his metaphor and it instantly ignited my epiphany about the problem. "I hear you," I said, "I really do." I had their full attention now. "But you know what? You don't get to go from being a boy to being a man just by sitting beside the men around the campfire. You can't jump from being a girl to becoming a woman just by putting on makeup and a business suit. Being taken seriously as a leader works the same way. You can't just play a role and dress the part. You have to earn that right!"

I went on to explain how mature leadership is not really about hitting a particular chronological age as much as it is about taking responsibility for your life, your business, and going on the hunt for yourself. When you stop relying on others or blaming others or waiting on others to go kill something and bring it back for you to eat, you realize you have to go hunt and kill for yourself. You don't complain about what you lack or let setbacks get in the way of finding a way to make your dreams happen.

You just go do it.

Once you've killed a few deals of your own, then you've gained the confidence and experience needed to go after bigger prey. You've earned the respect of others and shown you can handle dealing with the pressures and problems inherent in being a leader of your own business. You show that you know where you're going and have thought about how to land your plane. Other leaders and entrepreneurs then become willing to help you, guide you, and mentor you because they know the investment of their time and wisdom will not return void.

You can't expect to be considered a successful entrepreneur or experienced leader until you've moved beyond the thrill of the kill. Hunters not only have to know what they're looking for, where to find it, and how to kill it—they also have to know how to skin it, dress it, and cook it if they're going to survive and sustain themselves. Over time they develop the sensibilities and sensitivities necessary for long-term success.

Similarly, entrepreneurs determined to soar not only do what's necessary to get their plane off the ground, they also do what's essential to keep it airborne and to land it safely when the time is right. They know that soaring requires a pilot willing to show up every day who can confidently guide the plane toward the ultimate destination of success.

No matter what kind of weather or turbulence or unexpected passengers come your way, you, too, must remain in the cockpit and keep a steady hand at the controls. You must be committed beyond the initial impediments that inevitably occur in the early days of your venture. You must see your flight through to the finish!

Three Ts of Success

I tried not to chastise those young entrepreneurs or sound critical as I shared my thoughts on their predicament. I tried to encourage them by helping them see that the speed bumps they're facing are normal parts of the process and very necessary to their growth and maturity as entrepreneurs and as leaders. I reminded them that this is true of business as well as our character as well as our spiritual faith. The Bible tells us to "exult in our tribulations, knowing that tribulation brings about perseverance; and perseverance, proven character; and proven character, hope" (Rom. 5:3–4 NASB).

I stressed that the problem was not the way others regarded them but the way they regard themselves. The more they hunt or fly or whatever metaphor we want to use, the more they will be noticed by others in their fields and beyond. Instead of quitting and trying something else, they just need to relax and dig deeper. Perseverance refines our character and makes us stronger and wiser leaders. It reflects our ability to begin with the end in mind.

Many young men and women share the feelings expressed by this group regarding their entrepreneurial endeavors. Growing up in the Internet age, they're accustomed to entrepreneurs, many of whom are their peers, exploding overnight as viral sensations with millions of hits. They have friends who aren't even trying to sell anything who amass social media followers in the tens of thousands. Such instantaneous success appears to happen magically without slogging through the waiting, watching, and wondering phase that the vast majority must experience.

It's like the cooking shows you see on TV. The celebrity chef shares her recipe and walks you through making her dish in only ten minutes. Magically, her vegetables are already chopped, her butter is already at room temperature, and, of course, her perfectly equipped kitchen is clean and beautifully organized. And no sooner has she placed her pan in the oven than we see her taking a bite of the completely cooked entrée.

Even though we know she had that finished dish ready beforehand, along with lots of help from her production crew, we think we should be able to cook the same dish just as easily and quickly. I fear millennials often have the same kind of perfect-dish mentality with their careers and new ventures. When they struggle or aren't immediately recognized by others for their talent, they grow impatient and feel frustrated or disrespected.

If they persevere, however, they gradually realize that success requires talent *and* time *and* tenacity, the three Ts of success.

Power in the Process

There's another reason persevering and learning to solve problems is so essential for an entrepreneur's success. This process of growing in experience strengthens your ability to see where you're going and to adjust course as necessary based on variable conditions to ensure that your destination remains in sight. Most facets of wisdom can only enter our faculties through experience. There's simply no shortcut for success.

It's like learning to drive a car. You can read a textbook, study the owner's manual, and even pass a written test online. But until you sit behind the wheel, it's impossible for you to know exactly how your knowledge should be applied. You may know all the rules of the road, but you'll never reach your destination without putting the pedal to the metal!

Experience also forces you to become responsive to diverse and unexpected conditions. Focusing on promotion and marketing too soon happens with many new entrepreneurs because they're unable to look ahead and anticipate multiple outcomes. They lock in on their destination with only one route in mind, and when that route gets blocked, they don't know how to recalibrate their course.

Experienced pilots know they must adjust course all the time, sometimes in response to storms or rough air and other times due to heavy traffic from other planes in their shared airspace. Just because they change course doesn't mean they lose sight of their destination. They're still going to get their passengers to New York or Hong Kong or São Paulo, but they're going to improvise, adapt, and adjust based on changes.

Change should never surprise an entrepreneur—it must be anticipated so you can avoid problems that would slow you down and embrace opportunities for growth. New entrepreneurs may be naïve or too inexperienced to realize that their vision must extend forward all the way to their destination—the success of their business—and then work backward. Thinking first about the end result you want allows you to consider possible pitfalls and obstacles that might deter your momentum and impede your company's growth.

When you look at where you want to go, you can more accurately determine the best route to get there. Let's say your destination is Sydney, Australia, departing from North America. Knowing this is your starting point, you know you're either going to fly or take a boat, which in turn will greatly affect the timing of your arrival. Once you've chosen your means of transportation, then you can settle on a route. Whether it's direct or requires several transfers also affects your pace and arrival time.

Success for your business is the same. While we would all like to explode overnight into crazy success beyond our wildest dreams, that simply isn't likely or feasible for the vast majority of entrepreneurs. Yes, it does happen, largely thanks to social media and technology, but those success stories are exceptional, not normal. Count on cultivating your new venture over time, knowing you have much to learn through this process of experience, maturity, and growth.

Your power to reach your destination lies in the process!

Room to Grow

The entrepreneurs who become leaders in their field of endeavor know how to respond and adapt to conflicts and calamities, but they also know how to guide the variables over which they have influence. They realize early in the process what has to happen to get where they're going, and they work in that direction accordingly. They aren't afraid to change the size or shape of their plane in order to catch the best cultural currents. And they aren't too proud to take advice from others who have flown before them.

If you design your plane without room to grow, you will forever be a solo pilot. Many people approach me and describe their struggles to increase their business or expand their influence. But when I begin questioning them, it's clear that they've designed their business as something only they can control. Unwilling to hire talented people and invest in their employees' innovations for the company, these solo fliers create a bottleneck by forcing every individual, every team, and every department to have their approval before anything is done. Which, in essence, means that this entrepreneur runs a one-person business whether she has no employees or a hundred!

When you attempt to produce all products and determine all decisions for your company, you may enjoy a modicum of success, but you will never soar. Your professional ventures become contained by your personal limitations. You may know how to create certain products or offer particular services, but you won't know how to inspire others to join you or how to lead them to greater heights. It's fine to be a one-person band—and you can produce some pretty good music that way. But you'll never compose and perform a great symphony due to your inability or unwillingness to empower and direct an orchestra.

Independence alone is ineffective. In his book *The 21 Irrefutable Laws of Leadership*, the iconic business guru John Maxwell emphasizes that leadership is predicated on influence. Applying this axiom to entrepreneurs, clearly leadership cannot be exercised in isolation. Your influence needs to be exercised on a daily basis. Small businesses need loyal, repeat customers to endure. Once you begin hiring employees or subcontracting parts of your process you will need to influence these participants as well.

Entrepreneurial influence is not just about making a pitch or completing a sale. It's about how you brand yourself, promote yourself, and market your products and services. This kind of influence is reflected in your relationships and how you interact and become integrated within your community. Entrepreneurial leadership is ultimately measured in your ability to influence those around you in constructive, consistent, and coherent ways.

And let me remind you that this kind of influence goes much deeper than appearances. It's not only the message you communicate but also the way you communicate it. Perhaps more importantly for many new entrepreneurs, true leadership requires responsiveness. It necessitates actively listening and keenly observing all those around you and how they interact with you.

You don't get to control what you confront, but you do control your response to it. You may need to practice patience and cultivate self-discipline in order not to be riled or emotionally distracted by problems and personalities. You will have to find ways to express your point of view without undermining your ultimate objective. This means staying cool in high-pressure situations and not flying off the handle. Remember, sometimes the best thing you can say is nothing at all!

As an entrepreneur leading your business to growth and success, you also have to become accustomed to making decisions quickly and on the fly. You won't always have the luxury to wait on a thoroughly researched report or complete your usual due diligence. And you will naturally make mistakes along the way. But don't allow a past bad decision to inhibit you from acting decisively the next time you're faced with a crucial choice.

Avoiding Turbulence

Skilled pilots know how to avoid turbulence before they feel it. They have the advantage of technology, of course, but many of them also have learned telltale signs based on wind speed, weather patterns, and altitude. Entrepreneurs who become effective business leaders similarly learn how to avoid certain problems.

One of the most obvious ways good leaders create the best environment possible is by avoiding needless challenges. Reactions and responsiveness are often determined by forethought and preparation. I love leaders who are able to avoid chaos by managing situations before they develop into full-blown crises. As simple as it sounds, this often only involves thinking through the various possibilities and permutations of your business processes.

Successful entrepreneurs know better than to plan a picnic in a rain forest, but they also know to tuck their umbrella in the picnic basket on a sunny day. Storms can blow in when you least expect them. It's amazing how easily some problems can be avoided if some simple precautionary measures have been taken.

Effective leaders also maintain more than just a positive attitude—they cultivate a constructive attitude. What's the difference, you might ask? It's actually quite simple. People with a positive attitude hope for the best. People with a constructive attitude make the best of what they've got in order to get closer to where they want to be. In essence, it's the difference between planning and executing, between dreaming and doing.

If you are going to be a successful entrepreneur, you know that complaining, criticizing, and blame-shifting accomplish absolutely nothing. People who tend to whine about problems instead of finding ways through them are not really cut out to be entrepreneurs. And heaven help you if these people are your employees!

If your team members always bring you problems but not solutions, they may have titles or nice offices but they're not leaders. Sometimes such complaints can be a sign that you're not delegating and trusting them enough, but other times focusing on negatives reflects a passive mind-set. Such individuals expect others to take responsibility for causing change rather than creating change themselves.

I've hired many people for many enterprises who thought I was bringing them on board to maintain our current level or standard of service. What they don't realize is that if all we do is maintain what we have, there is no growth. All they see is the nursery and not the high school! Growth requires including others in your vision for where you're going. You wouldn't get on any plane and expect to land at your chosen destination. Similarly, you probably wouldn't get on a plane and willingly allow the pilot to take you wherever he or she wanted. No, we want to be informed of our destination and plan accordingly what's required to get there.

Growth requires dynamic change. Rarely do I hire anyone to simply maintain an asset and keep things where they are. Even if I hire a gardener to repeat his performance from the previous season, he still has to consider how conditions have changed with the soil, the weather, and the property before he can begin to improve the landscaping and overall appearance. This principle holds true in virtually any endeavor, whether you're starting a new business, a new church, or a new family.

In many couples, one person is satisfied to stay where they were while the other wants to see some level of progress in exchange for their relational investment. There's nothing worse than leaving the ground and heading toward the clouds only to realize you're still anchored to your hangar! How will your new venture ever soar if it's tethered by the timidity of the individuals to whom you entrust its maintenance and care?

While we all may not pursue improvement at the same speed, I'm convinced all of us crave it. We're made to increase our investments and improve our conditions on every level. No pilot sets out to miss his destination and crash-land elsewhere. A church planter doesn't set out to create an empty sanctuary. A child isn't raised to remain at a first-grade level. An entrepreneur doesn't invest his or her energy in an endeavor intending to lose money.

You will always increase the likelihood of your success if you consider how to land before you take off!

CHAPTER 9

Fail Fast and Crash Last

Entrepreneurial Leadership 102

Failure is another stepping-stone to greatness.
—Oprah Winfrey

It was a cold, overcast January afternoon like so many others at New York's busy LaGuardia Airport. Inside the terminal, US Airways Flight 1549 boarded passengers for its almost full flight, a total of 155 people including the crew. They were headed to Charlotte's Douglas International Airport before continuing across the country to Seattle. Like most commercial flights out of New York, Flight 1549 served a mixture of professional and business passengers along with individuals and family members traveling to visit relatives or reunite with loved ones at home.

It should have been a typical flight on a Thursday afternoon. But as the plane taxied down the runway, no one on board could imagine what would transpire in the next five minutes. Before the plane reached an altitude of three thousand feet, it encountered a massive flock of Canada geese, which bombarded the plane hard enough to take out both engines. Suspended in air only a few miles from Manhattan, the passengers' goose was cooked!

Emergency Landing

It was no laughing matter, however, when the pilot and his copilot realized they didn't have enough power to return to LaGuardia or the next closest airport, New Jersey's Teterboro. They would have to make an immediate decision, one that would determine whether everyone on board lived or died. The pilot, a silver-haired gentleman in his late fifties by the name of Chesley "Sully" Sullenberger, knew their only hope was an emergency landing on the softest, least populated surface available. He would need to glide the plane into the Hudson River beneath them (www.sullysullenberger.com).

Which, as you likely recall, is exactly what he did! With experience flying gliders as well as fighter planes back in his Air Force days, Sully knew exactly what he was doing as he guided the massive mechanical monolith, with the help of First Officer Jeffrey Skiles, into a controlled ditching on the surface of the cold, murky Hudson. With the aid of crew members, all passengers disembarked and were rescued within minutes by teams in boats large enough to carry them safely to shore.

Sully was the last one off the plane after twice checking to make sure everyone else had vacated. He had sacrificed the plane but saved its most precious cargo. There were no casualties and only a handful of serious injuries. Considering the tragedy that could have easily unfolded, reporters quickly dubbed it the "Miracle on the Hudson" thanks to the fast thinking, courage, and skill of Sully and his crew.

Later, reflecting on how so much of his professional and personal experience had prepared him for that event, Sully said, "One way of looking at this might be that for 42 years, I've been making small, regular deposits in this bank of experience, education and training. And on January 15, the balance was sufficient so that I could make a very large withdrawal" (Bill Newcott, "Wisdom of the Elders," *AARP Magazine*, p. 52). Without a doubt, Sully was uniquely qualified to do what had to be done to save lives and minimize injuries on Flight 1549.

Can you imagine being on that flight? I don't even like flying over bodies of water so I can only imagine what it would be like to land there! But I do know what Sully demonstrated in that life-or-death situation is the same kind of courage under fire you will need if your business is to soar. Because there will always be obstacles, challenges, and detours in the path of your trajectory. Who would have suspected that something as benign as geese could bring down an entire plane?

Improvisation in life's crises is a skill we must all practice and hone long before calamity strikes. It requires preparation, engagement, resourcefulness, and creativity to come up with solutions when your new business faces potential disaster. But the best entrepreneurs, like the best pilots, can land gracefully even in the most challenging of circumstances. In this chapter we'll explore some of these landing strategies to help you overcome problems that can be expected as well as ones that cannot be predicted.

Wing It and Bring It

One of the first problems most entrepreneurs face is their own impatience and unfamiliarity with the stop-and-start, hurry-up-and-wait, trial-and-error nature of the process involved in starting a new venture. While we can do our best to create lists, sequential time lines, and organizational charts, when you're launching your business you may have to wing it until you can bring it. In other words, we must have clear targets, goals, and systems while remaining flexible enough to adapt to the realities of business as we discover them.

A big part of this is simply cultivating courageous patience within yourself. While it's nothing compared to what the passengers on Flight 1549 went through, I absolutely hate being on a plane when it's stuck on the runway. Whether it's before takeoff or after landing, there's nothing worse than that limbo of inactivity without progress toward your destination. There's nothing more painful than sitting still when you should be flying! No one likes stagnating rather than exercising their freedom of movement. I fear too many new entrepreneurs return to the runways, longing to take flight again and strengthen their wings but grounded by their fears, their failures, and their frustrations. Or they rush back into flight too quickly without learning the lessons revealed by their previous airborne experience.

Gradually, you will discover your pace and rhythm, the busy seasons and the slow cycles of your business. Make peace with the fact that you're creating a new pattern while attempting to fulfill the business blueprint you have created. Once again, let me state emphatically that problem-solving is essential to being an entrepreneur. It's simply part of the inherent process of testing, trying, experimenting, adjusting, researching, and regrouping. Most successful entrepreneurs know that perseverance is essential to overcoming setbacks and continuing toward your destination of success.

If it's the word *failure* you're hung up on, then use the term Oprah used in the quotation at the beginning of this chapter—a *stepping-stone* to your future success. A stepping-stone is merely a mile marker between where you are and where you're going—it's never your destination! Stepping-stones bridge one educational opportunity to another so that you can move forward, even if it's a smaller leap than you once hoped. Sometimes stepping-stones are lateral moves and don't advance you at all; sometimes they require you to step back and regroup before leaping forward again. But all of them provide you with a transitional perch, with airspace where you can keep going until weather conditions change or new routes reveal themselves.

You see, failure can always be mitigated if you're willing to change both your attitude and your perspective on the catalyst driving your fears. As difficult as it may be to separate our emotions from our business, we must find a place to channel and express our feelings outside of the office, boardroom, studio, or workshop. If the Wright brothers had lost confidence in their abilities after their first model crashed, they would not have continued to redesign and retest all the variations that eventually lifted them off the ground. If Captain Sullenberger had panicked in the moments following the realization that his plane had no engines, he might not have been able to come up with the amazing solution that formed in his mind.

Think of the countless entrepreneurs who have tirelessly tackled, tinkered, tweaked, and teased different aspects of their business model until they discovered the perfect blend for their market. From Colonel Sanders's kitchen producing his secret recipe of eleven herbs and spices to Mark Zuckerberg's dorm room at Harvard launching what we now have as Facebook, most entrepreneurs enjoy the process of bringing their products to market as much as they enjoy selling them. Steve Jobs, the cofounder and CEO of Apple, once said, "I'm convinced that about half of what separates the successful entrepreneurs from the non-successful ones is pure perseverance" (https://www.entrepreneur.com/article/240047).

Just as you must make a deliberate decision to move forward, to get your engines revving, your propellers turning, to speed down the runway if you ever want to get off the ground, you must also be intentional about doing what it takes to stay in flight until you're ready to soar. I encourage you to frequently—weekly or even daily— identify your current location and present altitude and compare them to where you want to be going. Depending on variable market and production conditions, don't be afraid to change your route and approach your goal from a different direction.

Many new entrepreneurs suffer most, ironically, from being successful too early in their ascent. Getting too many unexpected orders too fast can ruin your business. I remember discovering a woman who baked the most delicious cakes and sold them from her website. Her homemade pound cake melted in my mouth, and after my first bite I knew right away I had found the perfect Christmas gift to send to friends and colleagues. Unfortunately, however, she could not handle the volume of cakes I needed sent before the holidays arrived. She had dramatically underbudgeted and understaffed production going into the holiday season.

Remember, a blessing too fast is no blessing at all! You have to know your capacity, and that means identifying your limitations and liabilities. This level of awareness also entails knowing exactly who your ideal customer is and everything about her. Such knowledge will help you anticipate product demand and sales cycles, which in turn can influence the way you manage inventory and handle marketing.

Blow Out the Candles

If you begin with baby steps before you try to run, you will often avoid the falls and spills to which most toddlers are prone. For instance, no matter how good the discounted price may be for a bulk order of your customized product, do not place that order until you have seen, felt, tasted, touched, and used the product for yourself. Many entrepreneurs quickly discover it's more cost-efficient to produce their product, or certain components of it, overseas. While outsourcing production is a part of many successful businesses, you want to be sure nothing gets lost in translation. Whether it's a language barrier or a cultural practice, you want to anticipate potential misunderstandings before they derail your order.

My wife, Serita, learned this lesson when she decided to test the market for one of her favorite home décor items. She absolutely loves candles and would probably burn them in every room all the time if it were up to her! After years and years of shopping, purchasing, and burning dozens of brands, scents, and sizes of candles, she decided to try her hand at creating her own. She loved comparing the different ingredients and learning about the differences between wax and soy, along with the hundreds of possible scents and varieties of wicks.

Who knew something so simple had so many options?

A good entrepreneur does, that's who!

Serita quickly learned the second most frequently asked question investors pose to participants on *Shark Tank*: What are your raw costs? How much are materials? What about production and labor? Packaging and shipping? Having an accurate per unit cost for your products or services is paramount to your success. In order to make the decisions that determine your cost, which in turn directly affects your retail price to consumers, you must know, as specifically as possible, what kind of product yours will be and who will buy it. Timex is not competing with Rolex although both make watches. Manolo Blahnik and Payless both sell shoes but not usually to the same clientele.

My wife studied the candle market and discovered what she already had learned as a consumer: it costs considerably more to make the smokeless, beautifully scented, long-burning elegant candles than the smoky, drippy, foul-smelling, fast-melting kind. Despite the higher production cost, she decided that she wanted to create and sell the same kind of candles she herself enjoys purchasing and burning. This decision meant using higher-quality materials that increased unit costs, which also elevated the retail price. And the kind of person willing to spend forty bucks on a candle is not the same kind looking to spend four bucks on one! Serita realized she would be competing with high-end retailers such as Neiman-Marcus, Anthropologie, and Nest, not Target and Yankee Candle.

Similarly, Walmart doesn't sell Chanel handbags or Armani suits. Not because they can't but because they have decided who their client is and researched what their client is looking for. Consequently, they are committed to staying within the confines of their target customer's budget, which typically does not include high-end designer brands and luxury items. They know that price points must match the target audience. When I talk to executives at KFC, Sam's Club, and Walmart, they tell me they look at the median income of the communities within a reasonable driving radius from each store location in order to project how much they will sell in that region. This information also helps them decide which specific products and brands to carry in that particular locale.

You can't be everything to everyone so don't try. Simply know where you are, what you can do, who your customer is, and what they want. One of the biggest mistakes I see entrepreneurs making is casting their customer nets wide but not deep. Decades ago such an approach might have been effective at catching consumers, but not anymore. Today we have choices upon choices regarding virtually every product and service available. As a result, customers expect to find the perfect product, solution, or service for their particular personal need, taste, and budget.

Focus in on where you are and what you have to build upon and try to avoid everything that's peripheral. Don't be distracted by what your business is not; be fully engaged with exactly all that you intend your business to be. Yes, it's tricky, because you have to keep one eye on where you are and all that's going on around you with current conditions while at the same time keeping your other eye looking ahead and beyond to your ultimate destination.

Acting Your Age

Another common setback many new entrepreneurs encounter is the limitation of their generational perspective. So often we forget the age-related cultural lens through which we view our world, but it can have a dramatic effect on how we approach and execute our business plan. Depending on our target, we may need to see beyond our own experience to understand the rationale and buying habits of customers older or younger than ourselves.

Just consider how someone growing up in the 1960s and '70s differs in their experience of life compared to someone coming of age in the 1980s and '90s! From social, political, and economic conditions to popular preferences in music and media, each generation typically defines itself in ways distinct from preceding ones. Some differences may be radical and reflect shifting values, such as views on dating and marriage, while others are more subtle and personalized, such as the appeal and impact of a culture-saturating film like *Star Wars*.

I've often attempted to share wisdom in the form of constructive criticism with many millennial entrepreneurs, but they are by no means the only ones limited by their generational perspective. So allow me to address my peers and other older nonmillennials and point out the most common problem we older entrepreneurs often encounter.

Just as I learned from watching my parents, many baby boomers assumed that any successful business required long hours, hard work, self-discipline, and limitless patience. We saw members of the Greatest Generation scrimp, save, and sacrifice in order to put food on the table and keep their families together. We emulated their work ethic with a fierce determination to get ahead at any cost and transcend the hardships and heartaches that often plagued their economic realities. We became more independent and self-sufficient, reluctant to ask for help, admit our need, or accept assistance from others willing to give aid.

But our fierce tenacity—our kids would say stubbornness!—often leaves us with a prideful blind spot. We have the guts and grit to be tenacious about launching our dreams but often lack the knowledge to use the gadgets, apps, social media, and software that can expedite the process. Our blind spot is to think that our effort replaces the efficiency of contemporary technology! Which sounds silly when we stop and think about it, because that's the whole point of technology—doing complex functions faster than human capabilities can. We know this cognitively, but we're still living in the 1980s!

If we mix our guts with younger generations' gadgets, however, we can reach greater altitudes of success much faster. Using such a potent combination, we can reduce overhead and improve our income as social media enables us to target our approach and sustain connection with our followers, fans, and customers. We can forgo the exorbitant expense of generalized marketing methods in print and on radio and television. When using these now almost old-fashioned methods, one paid according to the number of households the media reached—the reader circulation, listener radius, or viewing shares of the particular station or network.

But, of course, not every household holds your target customers. Social media affords you the luxury of identifying your constituents, connecting with their interests, and building long-term relationships that can be used to sustain your business and expand your vision. You can provide relational value and ongoing community that makes selling your products and services a much more organic exchange than it once was.

I recommend that you start by considering how many businesses and entrepreneurs you follow on Twitter, Facebook, Instagram, or some other social media (and if you're not following successful entrepreneurs online, then put this book down and do so immediately!). Which ones not only inform you but also make you *feel* something when you read their blog, email, post, text, or tweet? Which ones do you actually enjoy and look forward to reading and engaging with? What is it these other entrepreneurs are doing to strengthen their bond with you? And more importantly, how can you transfer this and scale it to your own use and advantage?

Yes, we boomers can learn a lot by using the millennials' technological savvy, and they can benefit from our gutsy grit and tenacity. Our children and grandchildren have benefited from our hard work but unintentionally have assumed certain unreasonable expectations because they typically haven't had to work as hard as their parents. So many of us have struggled and earned what we have by pulling ourselves up by our bootstraps in pursuit of our American dream. But now millennials feel entitled to the same—or greater—levels of success without having to do all that we did to get there. Even those who don't feel entitled can't always seem to estimate the effort it takes to get what they want.

At the Movies

You have to look ahead to your ultimate destination with one eye and keep the other focused on your next step. Remember that graduation is rooted in the word *gradual*. Most of the time you must pick up speed before advancing to the next level at a higher altitude.

Leaping into something without already knowing the capacity of your engine is usually ill-advised. Until you respect where you are, you cannot inspect where you're going.

Don't climb too high too fast—the liftoff should never surprise the pilot! Good pilots have been picking up ground speed, warming up all engines, making sure their wings are angled at the correct position to catch present wind conditions. Similarly, you must know the ground speed necessary to leave your present job, find a location, market your product or service, and start your business. You will need to have a threshold or tipping point as an indication of when to expand or when to cut back.

Up-to-date research, candid conversations with competitors willing to talk to you, and wisdom from your mentors can go a long way in helping you understand the quirks and idiosyncrasies of your customers and market. For example, I learned early on, thanks to the wisdom of generous mentors, that when our church reached 70 percent capacity, it was time to go to a second service. Knowing when to adjust velocity is crucial for smooth takeoffs without lurching and lunging off the runway.

Here's another example from my experience. Early in the process of producing feature films, I had to make choices concerning the costs and kinds of films I wanted to make. Considering various business plans, I quickly realized that most Hollywood movies carry a hefty price tag, which probably averaged around $75 to $100 million at the time. Even partnering with a large, established media giant such as Sony, I did not wish to risk this kind of capital on a new venture notorious for being fickle.

I also learned that certain types of films—namely, genres like fantasy, science fiction, and action/adventure—cost even more to make. These movies often rely on dramatic set pieces involving car chases, outer space voyages, and superhero battles that require lots of crashes, collisions, and CGI green screens. As you may know, many of these motion pictures have budgets in the hundreds of millions of dollars, which then require enormous worldwide box office just to break even.

My research led me to limit my budget to so-called smaller films with budgets under $50 million, usually between $15 and $30 million. In addition to not wishing to risk crazy-big money, I had little interest in telling those kinds of stories on screen. Instead, I was much more interested in stories involving family, faith, and friendship with a cast grounded in a realistic setting audiences would relate to and recognize. Within the industry, these genres are usually considered to be dramas, romantic comedies, or a hybrid known as "dramedy" in which there is considerable humor mingled with dramatic intensity. Such stories rely more on a talented screenplay being brought to life by a talented cast supported by a hardworking team than they do on special effects and over-the-top set pieces.

This approach has worked well for me and allowed me to produce amazing films such as *Woman, Thou Art Loosed!*, *Not Easily Broken*, *Jumping the Broom*, *Sparkle*, *Black Nativity*, *Heaven Is for Real*, and others screened in theaters in this country and around the world. While most of the movies I've produced are predominately about black characters and aimed at black audiences, I've always been mindful to include diversity. Something that moves you in a film transcends demographic lines, and funny is funny no matter what color you are!

Leading by Instinct

Another big issue that often forces new entrepreneurs to make an emergency landing is their style of leadership. A few years ago, I wrote a book called *Instinct* that focuses on—you guessed it—the way we can harness our instincts to improve our lives. Nowhere do instincts wield such considerable power than in the way you lead your business. Your instincts emerge as the offspring of all the objective data—both hard and soft, historical and current—married to your subjective experiences. Combining both intelligence and imagination, instincts fuel most entrepreneurs and their desire to do something new and different.

Instinctive entrepreneurs also know that if they cannot assemble a talented, unified team as their business expands they will always be limited by the kind of plane they can fly and the duration of their flights. No matter how talented you are or how hard you work, you can't do it all! You can't finance your business, produce as much product as needed, market it, promote it, distribute it, maintain it, and extend your company in new directions without relying on others. As an entrepreneur, you must learn when to ask for help and when to focus on what only you can do.

If you rely only on yourself, your income is limited by you being your only resource. If you want to be a great doctor, you can practice medicine in a number of skill- and career-enhancing ways—in hospitals, clinics, universities, and foreign aid programs. But if you want to be wealthy, successful, and expand your ability to bring healing to your immediate community, you will likely need to open up an office and hire additional doctors. Never forget that in the pursuit of hands-on businesses there will be a salary cap. The cap comes as you realize that no matter how fruitful and industrious you may be, you remain limited unless you can duplicate your capabilities and extend your vision to others.

Instinctive entrepreneurial leaders know how to prioritize and they pace themselves accordingly. Increasing the size of your business, influence, and income may not be as important as protecting your privacy, maintaining stability, and enjoying ample leisure time. You instinctively know what you want, so don't lead yourself and others to someone else's definition of success. You may prize independence over innovation. However, if your natural instinct for independence remains unchecked, you may not mature.

Independent entrepreneurs are often surrounded by many people willing to help but refuse to communicate their needs or to accept what others offer. Frequently, other people won't assist you in promoting and building your business because you look like you can handle it all by yourself. If you request help and enlist others willing to work with and for your business, you will be surprised how much healthier your business will become. On the other hand, if you send the signal that you don't need help, others will receive it accordingly.

Entrepreneurs inherently launch ventures that will grow enough to displace them from their initial roles. Anytime you can hone your talent and perform various skills you will always be able to work. But if you know *why* each task within your business must be tackled, you can delegate others to work for you! The why and the when of a task are inclusive for entrepreneurial leaders. In the beginning, you need to know what to do and when, but as your venture takes flight you discover the vital importance of knowing the whys and hows fueling your growth.

Your Next Runway

Once your new venture is airborne, your confidence will begin to grow. Then one day something will happen and suddenly you'll begin to doubt yourself more than ever. It might be a customer complaining or an employee criticizing your leadership. It could be an unexpected economic change that leaves you gasping for air as your business begins plummeting from the open skies where it previously sailed. Maybe it's simply the grueling demands of juggling sixteen-hour days seven days a week given family, friends, church, and other responsibilities.

Just as some problems can be anticipated as a normal part of the process, others can never be predicted. Unexpected events will always occur and threaten to send you crashing and thrashing back to ground level. Don't allow these nasty surprises or unexpected disappointments to ground you for long. Find a way to discharge any painful emotional baggage and look for the silver linings.

It's not how many times you have failed or how many stepping-stones you've been forced to traverse, it's what you've learned each time you get back off the ground! Did losing that customer help you change your customer service policy to one that has improved your business and attracted new clients? Did selling out of your handmade jewelry cause you to rethink the number of employees you need to meet demand? Did declaring bankruptcy for your last business enable you to manage your finances better for your new company? Each time you fail there's a clue to your future success.

You need to fail boldly if you want to succeed extravagantly! Successful people often do not reveal their failures—and why should they? We cannot fault them for not wanting to put their mistakes front and center, especially when they have clearly overcome those obstacles to reach the summits of their particular mountains. But you must remember that the person whizzing by you as you struggle to keep flying has experienced just as much turbulence as you have.

You have what it takes to pilot your business to greatness, but it may require a few emergency landings along the way. But don't be deterred, my friend. Repair your plane, get back in the cockpit, and head down your next runway!

PART IV

SOAR TO NEW HEIGHTS

Then you shall take delight in the LORD, and I will make you ride on the heights of the earth....

—Isaiah 58:14 ESV

CHAPTER 10

Growing Forward

Minding Your Own Business

If we're growing, we're always going to be out of our comfort zone.
—John Maxwell

I'm often questioned about what led to my decision to relocate my ministry and company from West Virginia to Texas. While many variables shaped that decision, one stands out that might be helpful to you as you confront the unique challenges that frequently accompany the growth of a new venture. Because you must realize that what got your plane off the ground is not necessarily what will sustain it in flight to your ultimate destination.

I had grown what started out as a very meager ministry from seven members to a body with about a thousand members and seven hundred in regular attendance. My company had started producing its own plays, and we were about to launch a tour. With a few best-selling books under my belt, I watched my literary career take off. For the area where I lived, and in the mind-set of those around me, I had done very well. I had a nice home, a beautiful family, a thriving business, and a growing church.

But from the pit of my stomach this feeling nagged at me, asserting that I had not maxed out my potential, that I had more in me than my current environment could accommodate. I wanted to start a ministry to the homeless and to those in prison and eventually launch an international outreach as well. Most of my comrades, bound as they were by traditional thinking about what a church could do and what a minister's role should be, were not thinking about such ancillary ministries at the time.

Perhaps their perspectives held merit, but my purpose refused to be incarcerated by others' perceptions. I knew my journey would be unique. If you can relate to this feeling, then I must warn you that uniqueness is seldom understood in real time. Little by little, I had to develop the courage to break outside the norms and commit to my convictions rather than my conditions. My vision had outgrown its environment, and a change was destined to take me from my homeland to my destined purpose. And as I soon learned, that purpose motivated my decisions in powerful ways.

Mind Your Metrics

Most organizations are fueled by profit, purpose, power, or by some potent combination of them in varying ratios. Most businesses run on a principle of profit, while ministries and charitable organizations operate on a priority of purpose. Political institutions and elected officials, on the other hand, are often driven by the pursuit of power.

While each of these three key motivators has a core ethic, all have traces of the others within them. If a nonprofit organization is consistently not profitable, then it cannot be sustainable. It's naïve to think you can focus solely on purpose without attending diligently to the facts and finances surrounding the goal that's been prioritized.

If a CEO's leadership consistently results in profitability for her company, then she will garner considerable power along the way. To ignore such power and its effect on future growth is to squander an opportunity for accelerating success. If an elected official exercises political power in ways that are not beneficial to their constituents, they will undermine their source of power. They must balance their role's power against the results attained for those they seek to serve.

Purpose, power, and profit each play a role in accomplishing what I like to call impact. When you consider impact, you're basically determining the level of results your efforts have on your department, company, community, city, and society. If impact is a quantifiable method of evaluating relevance, one cannot measure accomplishment without getting immersed in the metrics of success. Just as a short-distance runner needs a stopwatch to determine his ability to meet his goal in the 400-yard dash, one must be prepared to consider the specific metrics used to determine success.

Business success isn't measured by longevity alone. The fact that a business is sustained over a particular time period doesn't necessarily mean that it's profitable. Nonprofits cannot be measured by adherence to purpose alone because in order to remain functional they must make their payroll. Impact must be determined by a comparison of quantifiable metrics: How many people did we feed? How much did it cost us? How long can we operate this way? How does this fit with our projected budget for this month, this quarter, this year? Such questions require metrics to provide answers about an organization's impact.

If you want to continue to maximize your God-given potential, then you must evaluate your ultimate impact and the cost of growing forward. It's not enough simply to reach a certain altitude and settle for a plateau of status quo. Sustained growth requires minding your metrics.

Lifesavers

When I was a child, my parents always took us for road trips to visit our grandmothers, no quick journey when you consider it often took up to seventeen hours each way. The problem was that my dad didn't have much time off, and most it was spent getting there. Though I'm sure it was much more affordable to go by car, it wasn't just about the money, because the trade-off was that while we saved money we also lost the precious time.

There was also the issue of the old man's exhaustion and the possibility of him falling asleep at the wheel since he had been working right up until the time we left. His return on investment might have been high because he saved money, but his effort-to-impact ration (E2I) was quite low. From an E2I perspective, it was much better when we took a plane. Flying to Grandma's house didn't save money but it did save time. From an E2I perspective, making the decision to drive was a failure that resulted in two short overnight stays in Mississippi or Alabama and a quick trip back in time for my parents' return to work.

I have come to look at both my return on investment (ROI) and my E2I ratio when evaluating most major decisions. I ask myself, "Considering all that I will invest in this direction, will the return be commensurate with the energy I expend? Or should I put my efforts elsewhere and reconsider the value of my time and my energy for what will be returned?"

My parents' decision to drive instead of fly weighted the money they saved more than the time spent to get there. Flying would have cost considerably more money but would have saved time and effort. The trip by car took almost thirty-five hours just coming and going versus the five to six hours if we had flown.

While my parents made the decision based on what seemed most important to them at the time, in order to sustain growth you will reach a critical point where time and effort mean more than the money you save. How much is twenty-four hours of your life worth at this point? In business just as in life, time is our most precious commodity—irreplaceable and irretrievable.

Inspecting Your Impact

Over my adult life, I've often had a recurring dream in which I'm fighting some unknown and ominous foe. The really frightening thing, however, is that in my dream my punches feel powerless. No matter how hard or fast I throw my punch, my fist never fully connects with my target. The impact doesn't reflect the intensity of the effort with which my punch is thrown.

Many times we who work hard in real life experience a similar dilemma. It appears that no matter how much effort we expend, we don't seem to see any impact, whether on the business, the marriage, the ministry, or wherever we've aimed our punch. I'm not sure what the solution to the problem is in my dream state (except to wake up), but in life we can correct the problem by no longer expending our greatest effort in the wrong places. Misplaced priorities can cause your E2I ratio to be as powerless as an impotent swing at the monster in your dreams. Instead you must aim your efforts at the places within your target where you can have the greatest impact.

In a purpose-based nonprofit, you have to look at energy and income to perceive if you have truly had an impact that fulfills your purpose even when it doesn't appear so on your bottom line. To be sure, you can't ignore either, but to be truly successful as a charitable organization, purpose isn't the only metric that guides your decisions. Similarly, more and more corporations are finding that though they are in business to make money, they are seeing the benefit of the greater good, including purpose and community impact, as an objective beyond margins, debt ratios, and income viability.

Impact looks at the results of the energy, emotions, and effort expended to accomplish the work. But it goes deeper than simply how much was expended; it goes to the very different metric of how much was accomplished. This is why I find the E2I ratio, effort as compared to impact, such a crucial catalyst for making decisions that will sustain growth and propel me closer to my ultimate destination. For the amount of effort expended, you must identify the impact returned for your time and energy.

Most businesses focus primarily on ROI, return on investment, when evaluating their past growth and projecting their future expansion. ROI usually involves playing a numerical game that focuses exclusively on the financial return on the financial investment. But such an evaluation often ignores another consideration: the return on the energy expended (ROE). When one considers the ROE, we acknowledge that there's more invested in a dream's fulfillment than just dollars and shares. ROE forces us to consider the impact achieved in light of the time and effort required.

This principle plays out in our efforts in the gym. When we run on a treadmill or train on an elliptical machine, we typically get an electronic reading of the calories burned for the time spent exercising on that machine—basically, how much impact you had on calories burned for energy (time and effort) expended. One quickly learns that not all fat-burning exercises are created equal!

Similarly, the automobile's metrics often come down to engine efficiency for the horsepower delivered. This measurement is simply a way for the consumer to understand and compare one engine's ability with another. Without such quantifiable metrics, one would be left to compare vehicles solely on appearance but not on effectiveness.

Most people are happy to live their lives based on the superficial glimpses and cosmetic glances of success. As long as they appear successful, they don't have to consider that the engine of their business may not be efficient. The outside of their venture sparkles and gleams, but the venture can't sustain flight once it's off the ground.

The problem with operating your life without looking at the metrics is simple: you can't effectively evaluate which, out of the many initiatives you're pursuing, are working *for* you and which are working *on* you! Is your energy having impact or is it merely expended without a significant return? Impact determines success. How else will you feel accomplished if your only measurement is survival based or reliant only on appearances?

Talent Show

Whether it's stockholders, investors, partners, or even God Almighty wanting to see your metrics, you will always need accountability. Often when we're actually busy in the trenches doing the work, we don't devote enough time to wondering if our E2I is tracking correctly. Without accountability, there is no path to forward growth and profitability.

We often see this truth illustrated in the Bible. In fact, this principle is the subject of one of Jesus' most famous parables. In the Gospels of Matthew (25:14–30) and Luke (19:12–28), Jesus uses the parable of the talents to teach us what it means to invest our gifts for a greater purpose. In the parable, a business owner puts three of his servants in charge of his goods, giving each of them responsibilities according to their abilities while he's away on a trip. He makes it clear through his words that the servants' focus should be on investing the talents and not on when he will be returning.

When he finally returns home, the owner calls in the servants and assesses their performance and stewardship over what he had given to them. After meeting with the first two, the master is pleased. He judges the two servants as faithful because they invested their talents and returned profits. They put the talents to work, invested them, and doubled what the master had given to each of them.

Though they ended with different levels of accomplishment, both were successful, with a 100 percent increase from where they started. I've always found it noteworthy that success for them was not competitive but was based on the level of return for the initial amount each was given to invest. This remains vitally important for us today. We must understand that our success isn't a measurement to be compared to the success of others. Though not as profitable, the steward with four talents was just as successful as the one who was given ten.

It was a different story, however, for the third servant. He'd been given a single talent, but he did nothing with it. He was the one with the least to risk, which usually makes a person more willing to step out in faith, and yet he buried it. Explaining his rationale, this servant tells the master that he'd been afraid and didn't want to lose the master's money, so he buried his one talent for safekeeping. The master is furious, calling the servant evil and lazy. The servant had wasted the talent he'd been given, doing nothing and yielding no results. The master takes that one talent away and gives it to the servant who now has ten talents.

In this parable, Jesus reveals exactly what he wants us to do with the gifts and talents that God has given us. We are to be responsible for the gifts and the talents he has placed inside each of us, investing them for maximum return. It's important for us as entrepreneurs to understand this parable and see how it relates to our lives. We have all been given gifts and talents.

Seeds have been planted inside each and every one of us, though they have been given in different measures. All the seeds must be watered, all the seeds must be used, and all can potentially bear fruit. We cannot be like the third servant, just burying our gifts and talents because we're too afraid or too lazy or too uninformed to do with them what God wants us to do. Similar to what we see in this parable, God expects us to be faithful with what he's given us. He wants us to be responsible and to make sure the seeds we sow and the talents we invest yield profitable returns.

The parable of the talents reminds us that risk is necessary for growth to occur. Building a business with the seeds that have been planted inside of us, with the gifts and talents we've been given, enables us to fulfill our purpose in life and to enjoy contentment from doing what we were created to do. With the freedom that being an entrepreneur allows, we can help others maximize their own gifts and talents. We're able to do all of the things that God asks us to do and calls us to do because as entrepreneurs we are not bound to someone else's time, money, vision, or passion.

You don't have to sell Bibles or choir robes to invest your talents wisely for God's kingdom. In Luke 19:13, God tells us to "do business till I come" (NKJV). The order is clear. We're not to sit around, we're not to wait. He wants us to take action now. We have to occupy the world with businesses that are needed. We have to build businesses that are the answers to someone's prayers. We are to provide for and advance his kingdom.

And it doesn't matter what product or service you provide; it is the way that you do business that will make a difference. By having a business, by being in front of customers, you'll be able to share the message of the Gospel just by your actions. You will represent God in the way you operate, in the way you treat your customers and your employees. How you interact will be your message; how you communicate will show who you serve.

God wants you to use what he's given you in order to give you more. Being faithful in the small things and remaining diligent will generate winds of opportunity when you may least expect them. And when those winds come, you want to make sure your plane is ready to fly higher than before!

Always on the Move

No matter how much you achieve or how quickly or slowly your new venture takes off, you should always view growth as both a process and a part of your destination. You must always be looking ahead even while you're keenly aware of where you are with your business. Wherever your entrepreneurial pursuits take you, once you've established and sustained your initial flight pattern you're ready to consider your next horizon. You can then propel yourself to new dimensions and project yourself to a place of new opportunities beyond your current altitude.

You may be able to remain physically where you are but come up with innovative products, enhanced services, and new ways of increasing production. You may have to adjust mentally and emotionally to different conditions than when you began so as to discover and catch up to where your market currently resides.

Or you may have to do what I did and physically move to a new location. Depending on the kind of business, its size and location, you may be able to continue your present business as is and duplicate it in another location or through another channel. This can be tricky because you do not want to cannibalize business from your first endeavor in order to nourish your second or third wave. You want to keep your core business healthy and thriving so that if conditions change and it's not the right time for growth you don't lose the momentum you had.

Whether you have to move away from where you are physically or move away from where you are mentally, it will be an exercise in faith as you go after the dreams and desires that God has placed inside of you. You'll have to take risks and then take some more and then get comfortable with the way risks and growth go hand in hand. Risks are inevitable and necessary because the greatest rewards are the result of the greatest risks.

Doing something new and different means that you will have to step out of that box; you'll have to move away from how you've defined yourself, but especially away from how others have defined you. Some of the greatest people I've met are people who were willing to do something different, willing to propel themselves forward and move away from how they'd been defined in the past. They refused to remain in the box where everyone expected them to be and everyone expected them to stay.

That is the key—never allow the crowd to define you or confine you. People get used to seeing us in certain roles and only exercising certain capacities. In my situation, many people probably saw me only as a small-town pastor, and I could have easily given credence to anyone who questioned me about leaving West Virginia. Then, after being questioned, I could have been left with my own doubts. I could have started questioning my own goals and asking myself: Why would I leave a place that was so comfortable? Why would I venture out to the unknown? Why leave home for something so different from what I've known?

Once you start questioning yourself, more doubts will set in, and very soon you will find yourself stagnant, doing the same thing, remaining in the same place because you allowed the crowd to define you. It would have been easy for me to stay where I was and let the crowd and my situation become my jail cell. Again, not because that's how I viewed where I lived, but it would have become my prison because I would never have broken out to pursue those things I knew I was meant to achieve. I could have stayed locked up, never going beyond what everyone else thought I should do.

Instead I stepped out and moved to another part of the country. For you, it may be something like redefining yourself as you embark on your new venture. But whatever it is, growth will always require you to risk your comfort. To succeed in today's times, you have to move, continuously shifting how you see yourself, and be the one to define who you want to be and where you want to go.

Continue to imagine, continue to dream, continue to create. Even once you've achieved, continue to reimagine, dream new dreams, and create new opportunities, expanding on whatever you have built for yourself. The key to your launching pad is understanding that you and only you must define yourself because that will set your goals, your future, and your success in motion. And even though you alone are responsible, growth will eventually require you to enlist professional help.

This Calls for a Professional

If you want to grow your business, get the best professional help you can afford. Why? Because you can't afford not to! One of the reasons you may not be growing as rapidly as expected is because you have not enlisted the professionals you need in order to grow your business. It might be because you're trying to save money and learn new systems yourself, or it might be because you're still stuck in a mindset that views your business as too small or insignificant to enlist the services of attorneys, accountants, bookkeepers, and others.

Shifting into a higher altitude often requires creating consistent operating systems for optimum functional growth. Boundaries may have been blurred as you've poured everything back into your business with no real salary for yourself. The more you get in the habit of blurring the line between your personal finances and your business finances, the more difficult it will be to unravel them later.

It might be something you can do yourself if you have an aptitude for numbers and accounting, with a little help from the many online resources available. You can utilize financial software, and a quick search on the Internet could lead you to the software you need. Software systems exist to track almost every aspect of a business: inventory, warehouse management, accounts payable and accounts receivable, your customers, budgeting, payroll, human resources, on and on. Any kind of report that you need or any tracking that you should do, you'll be able to find the software for it, yet another advantage of our digital age.

You may find, however, that you have neither the time nor the patience to learn everything you should do for the financial ins and outs of your business. Unless your business is itself related to finance (you're a financial planner, an accountant, or a bookkeeper), this area may not be your strength. That is why many entrepreneurs hire professionals: a bookkeeper, tax attorney, or a certified public accountant (CPA), whatever your business needs. Most of these experts will likely have experience dealing with entrepreneurs who own their own businesses.

These professionals can lead you in the right direction and save you a lot of time. If finances are not your forte, having a professional guide you through this part of your business is a wise investment. Professionals can often help you come up with workable operating systems that allow you to pay yourself. They can assist you in drafting and sticking to a budget for the optimum health of your business.

You might be surprised how much energy you free up when you have someone else, a professional whom you trust, handling areas you know nothing about, such as state and federal taxes, Social Security, insurance, pensions, and reserve accounts. Don't wait until you feel like you're on an island alone, waiting for a financial tsunami to overtake you. Getting professional financial help is often a catalyst for new growth and can assist you in making sure the financial side of your business is healthy and strong.

Follow the Money

While it is always smart to bring into your business professionals who can complement your strengths, when it comes to the money never turn over all financial responsibilities to any one person—especially when it comes to writing the checks. This is your business and you must have the ultimate control over it all, especially your finances. Your eyes have to remain on the books, even if this isn't something you want to do, even if you don't enjoy doing it, even if you feel that it will take up too much of your time—you have to be the one to maintain control. So much growth comes back to simple, obvious practices like sticking to your budget and investing some of your profits back into your business.

If you do allow someone else to sign the checks, I recommend having two signatures, and even with that you must review your books on a very regular basis. There are a multitude of horror stories of people who would have had successful businesses but instead had to close their doors because someone stole their money.

Issues such as embezzlement and theft often occur when the owner turns her back to the financial side of the business, but not all losses are related to dishonest practices. As the owner, when you're signing the checks, you will quickly see issues that arise. Why is the cost of goods going up? Why are our expenses so high this month? You will be able to handle problems as soon as you see such issues arise in your various accounts. Any successful person will tell you to sign your own checks, and when you're doing that everyone else will realize that you're minding your business.

And ultimately that's what growth is all about—minding your own business!

CHAPTER 11

The Miracle of Marketing

Burning Your Bushel to Fly Higher

I've learned that people will forget what you said, people will forget what you did, but people will never forget how you made them feel.

—Maya Angelou

Having grown up in the Space Age, I loved watching the movie *Hidden Figures*. Based on the nonfiction book of the same title by author Margot Lee Shetterly, the story reveals the dramatic and vital role African American women played in supporting NASA's space program and its successful efforts during the 1960s. Basically, these women, known as "computers in skirts," worked as mathematicians and engineers alongside the more visible white males attempting to lead the program. Without these fiercely determined women, however, it's likely the space program as we know it would never have existed!

In the film, we see Oscar-winner Octavia Spencer portraying Dorothy Vaughan, the first black supervisor at NASA. Working when segregation was still enforced, Vaughan demanded that her title reflect the actual supervisory work she was already doing.

Captivated by the premise of her character's struggle, Spencer at first thought the story was fiction. "And then when I realized it wasn't fiction," she said in an interview, "it was even more imperative to be a part of the story. They were highly educated and they were moms and they were dreamers and they had fierce natures. And so there was so much about who they were that wasn't lost on me" (http://www.npr.org/2016/12/16/505569187/hidden-figures-no-more-meet-the-black-women-who-helped-send-america-to-space).

These women were not satisfied with accepting the status quo and remaining at home in the kitchen or working in the socially acceptable roles dictated by segregation. They knew they were just as capable and intelligent, if not smarter, than any of their colleagues. They wanted to exercise their gifts and fulfill the God-given potential they had to participate in something that would change history forever.

In other words, these women were definitely entrepreneurs!

Entrepreneurial Evolution

These strong, driven women were part of an entrepreneurial evolution that had started decades earlier with the Wright brothers and other pioneers of flight and that culminated with Apollo 11 successfully fulfilling its mission on July 20, 1969. I remember as a boy watching Walter Cronkite on the evening news proclaim that we had landed on the moon and that two of the astronauts, Neil Armstrong and Buzz Aldrin, had actually *walked* on the moon's surface and planted our Stars and Stripes there to signal our triumph in being the first nation to accomplish such an astounding feat.

What had once been fodder for imaginative tales of science fiction about spaceships and little green men became a reality that fulfilled the promise of early pioneers of flight such as the Wright brothers. You see, Apollo 11's launch from the Kennedy Space Center in

SOAR!

Florida to the moon went through Kitty Hawk! If the Wright brothers had never invented a flying machine that, controlled by a pilot, could take off and sustain flight, who knows when or even if we would ever have made it into outer space and onto the moon.

While it might have been tempting to be satisfied with flying planes from continent to continent, entrepreneurial visionaries kept pushing the boundaries of known science until they reached new heights. Today those boundaries continue to be stretched as commercial space flights are becoming reality. Private companies such as Virgin Galactic, SpaceX, and Blue Origin have been pursuing commercial human spaceflight for the past two decades. At the time I'm writing this, they, along with several other corporate ventures, continue to develop programs that will transport members of the public into the cosmos (http://www.space.com/24249-commercial-space-travel-blasts-off-2014.html).

Can you imagine it? In our lifetime, we may be shuttling into space for our next vacation! But when such a possibility becomes as commonplace as Uber, it will have been because of a relentless determination to excel beyond expectations. It will have been because passionate entrepreneurs refused to settle for "good enough" and instead became the best. And for entrepreneurs trying to take their businesses to the next level, the best rocket fuel I know is to intensify your marketing efforts.

Marketing makes the magic that can transform your airplane into a rocket ship!

Missional Marketing

While we've touched on the vital importance of marketing already, I believe effective marketing is so paramount to the ultimate success of your business that I now want to expand how you think about it. While you may understand its importance for launching your business, I fear too many new entrepreneurs underestimate the significance marketing has in sustaining flight and reaching their destination. Learning to market effectively is an ongoing educational process and requires keen attention to cultural trends, exact timing, and customer relations.

Marketing is inherent to the process of being a successful entrepreneur. I fear many small business owners consider marketing a burdensome, necessary chore they must do to keep their business running, much like filling out tax forms or taking the trash out. But the best marketing is organic and integrated into who you are, what you're selling, why you're selling it, and who you're trying to reach. The best marketing efforts become synonymous with your brand even as they extend, enhance, and enforce it.

At the risk of being immodest or overestimating my own brand, I'll use myself as an example. When you picked up this book, chances are good that you had heard of me before you saw my name on the cover. Perhaps you have seen me on television or heard me preach when you visited The Potter's House. Maybe you recognized me from a conference you attended or from one of the many corporate events at which I speak. You might have read some of my other books, listened to music I produced, or seen my name rolling in the credits of a movie you watched.

Whatever it may have been, you likely had certain associations and preconceived notions of who T. D. Jakes is and what he's all about. These elements shaped how you perceive a product, like this book, with my name on it. More importantly, these factors also influence what you expect to receive from reading a book I've written on this topic. My publishers call this a book's "reader benefit" or "felt need"—basically, the benefits and payoff you will receive from a particular book.

If you didn't know that I'm an entrepreneur in addition to being a pastor, then you might wonder what I might possibly know about starting a new business and why it would apply to you. But at this stage of my career, I suspect most people who know me realize that I'm interested in a variety of topics in many diverse media, which leads me to keep a number of entrepreneurial irons in the fire.

While I have never set out to brand myself singularly as an entrepreneur, that umbrella covers my many interests and ventures quite well. In fact, I would caution you against being too narrow with your brand identity and marketing efforts because you want to leave room for growth and expansion—possibly in areas that may not occur to you when starting out. Instead, consider finding a way to incorporate your mission into your marketing.

Early on in my career, I realized that everything I do—from ministry to music to movies and beyond—revolves around my desire to inform, inspire, and entertain. I believe lives can be changed and transformed through those three relational pillars so I have built my ministry, my conferences, my books—everything I do—around making sure they all reflect enlightening information, innovative inspiration, and exceptional entertainment.

Burn Your Bushel

One of the stories that has most influenced my approach to branding and marketing occurs in Scripture. One day while I was reading the Bible, it occurred to me that Jesus preached one of his longest messages to five thousand men, not to mention wives, children, and other family members, but not one word in the text tells us what he said! The entire focus is on what he *did*:

> Taking the five loaves and the two fish and looking up
> to heaven, he gave thanks and broke the loaves. Then he

gave them to the disciples, and the disciples gave them to the people. They all ate and were satisfied, and the disciples picked up twelve basketfuls of broken pieces that were left over. The number of those who ate was about five thousand men, besides women and children. (Matthew 14:19–21)

Talk about one big picnic! Think about it—he took one boy's lunch of bread and fish and turned it into more than enough to feed thousands of hungry people. It seems so striking to me that we don't know what he taught or preached on specifically that day, but we do know what he served for lunch! His impact was in the miracle and that became his message. He had no Internet, radio, television, or even a flyer. But when he fed the five thousand, the message of the Messiah went everywhere. Thousands of people left there that evening talking about Jesus and what he had done for less than the price of a Happy Meal!

I suspect this miracle occurred relatively early in Jesus' public ministry. He obviously had a reputation because earlier in this passage (Matt. 14:13–14) we're told he tried to slip away and have some downtime. But crowds followed him and he had compassion on them and ended up healing the sick and injured. So between healing them and feeding them, word was out about who he was and what he could do.

No longer was his candle hiding under a bushel! What do I mean by that? Referring to the way we are to share our faith with those around us by what we do and say, Jesus later explained, "Neither do men light a candle and hide it under a bushel!" In other words, if we have the light we shouldn't hide it where no one can see it. I suspect there wasn't that much talk about Jesus or his ministry, not on a large scale at least, before he fed the five thousand.

As audacious as it might sound, I believe this miracle of marketing succeeded in spreading the Good News Jesus came to bring better than anything else he could have done. No longer was he just the carpenter's son from Nazareth—he was the all-powerful, grace-bearing, miracle-performing Son of God! Now that's getting the word out!

A Beautiful Strategy

As entrepreneurs, we must also find the best way to burn through the bushel that prevents our customers from seeing our candle. You must dispel the secrecy that threatens the success of your business and get the word out about who you are and what you have to offer. Otherwise, no matter how talented you may be or how incredible your product, service, or cause it's all for nothing because no one knows about it.

What good is it to be smart enough to write a book that no one reads? Or to start a real estate firm that potential customers can't locate? Or a catering service that hungry event planners don't know exists?

No matter what you're trying to do, if your product can't find its audience or your audience can't find your product, your business loses. It isn't enough to have a noble cause or an amazing product if you can't burn the bushel that separates you from your intended audience.

Hash tags, niche marketing, and doing analytics on the audience you are trying to reach is critical. You can spend a ton on advertising, but if it doesn't reach your demo you just wasted that money. It's like selling swimwear to a station that advertises in Anchorage! And who wants to advertise birth control in an AARP magazine?

Knowing who your audience is and where to reach them helps you target limited dollars to a select group.

You have to find a way to create an impression with the right people—potential customers and others who may be interested or can help get your word out. And you don't need to spend a lot of money to hit your bull's-eye. In fact, with creative thinking and a strategic approach, sharply focused marketing can also save you a ton of money.

For example, several years ago when we were marketing *Jumping the Broom*, a dramedy that I produced with Sony Pictures, they went high with limited dollars to TV and radio while I chose a different strategy and began targeting beauty shops. Since we had a predominantly black cast, I focused our impact on a strategic, concentrated audience.

I knew that women in our community use the beauty shop as their country club so I planned accordingly. The local beauty parlor is where all the neighborhood gossip spreads and the community news gets discussed. So we made *Jumping the Broom* aprons for beauticians and stylists and gave them as gifts at our early screenings. The buzz went crazy with a specific audience!

Brand Aid

Once you've launched your business and are trying to soar to the next level, it's a good idea to revisit your branding and marketing strategy. Why fix something that's not broken? Because the branding and marketing strategy that got you in the air is not necessarily going to keep you there or fuel your ascent into higher altitudes of success. Use what you've learned so far to refresh your messaging and make it more personal, more accurate, more "you." And use what you've learned about your customers to find them and engage them with laser-like precision.

Revisit the basics of your marketing message and force yourself to come up with new answers. Your brand image should reflect your company's message—after takeoff is yours still aligned? Or is there a gap that needs closing between the conceptual and the tangible? What is it *specifically* that you want to convey to your market about your business? What is the story that you want to tell? What is it that you want potential customers and clients to know about you and your company? What is that you want them to believe about you? What values do you want to communicate to customers? These questions can provide you with a marketing checkup exam to make sure that your new venture remains healthy and continues to grow beyond your launch.

Now that you have established a foundation for your brand, it's time to build on it. If it's shaky and needs reinforcement, then add the necessary support pieces to make your message and mission clear and memorable. While you will likely have chosen a name for your business at this stage, make sure that it truly fits your product and target audience. For instance, I once met a young woman who had just opened a day spa and named it after herself: Lapastii Ater Soror. Although the meaning behind the name—"beautiful black sister"—was wonderful and the way she pronounced it was lovely, she quickly realized it was a barrier to her business. Consequently, a few months after opening, she made the wise decision to change the name of her spa to Oasis.

I'm not sure why the young lady chose to name her business after herself initially, perhaps because it was convenient or expedient, but I know it didn't fit any of the criteria for a good business name. It wasn't easy to pronounce, wasn't easy to spell, and definitely wasn't easy to remember! It didn't communicate the specific kind of business nor did it deliver any kind of resonant, emotional message. I think it's safe to say that unless she was fortunate enough to have several celebrities talking about her spa and teaching the general public how to say that name, her new business would have continued to struggle.

To help you determine if your name and brand are having the impact you want, ask repeat customers and others you know well for honest feedback. The young lady who changed the name of her spa finally realized it wasn't working when a customer jokingly suggested she change the spa's name to something others could pronounce.

Remember: *your messaging begins with the name of your business.*

Tame the Name Game

If your original name isn't working or can be sharpened to clarify your message and brand identity, then change it before more time passes. Brainstorm new ideas and then revisit your original list of names and ideas for what to call your business. I understand your reticence to change your company's name after you've already launched it, but if it's not catching hold and connecting with customers, it's better to make a change now while your business is still alive than to wish you had made the change when it's too late.

Reflect on the names of businesses you like and focus on what in particular you like. Are they clever and involve wordplay, such as a shoe shop called Heart and Sole? Do they pique your curiosity with an appeal to something unique or exotic, such as a travel boutique called Bon Voyage? Maybe it's pure simplicity and clarity that you like, something we see in Brown Girls Books, the name of a small independent publisher started by two African American women.

Having the right name for your business is one of the most

important steps for growth and shouldn't be taken lightly. This name represents you in the public sphere, and much like Jesus feeding the five thousand, you want impact that will not only capture what you're offering to the public but a name that will deliver your message and if possible your values. You're not just naming a business; you're establishing your brand.

When providing branding consultation services to entrepreneurs about business names, a consultant of a major branding company says he first asks clients, "Do you want your company's name to fit in or to stand out?" The answer seems obvious, right? What business owner wouldn't want her company to stand out? Sometimes, however, this consultant cautions, new businesses entering certain industries—insurance, elder care, financial planning—might need a more conservative, "serious"-sounding name. A name that's wildly original in certain fields might not be taken seriously by prospective clients in other, more conservative arenas.

For the majority of new businesses, however, your name as well as your brand should be distinct, standing out from your competitors. You want it to be clear and concise but also to have an element of surprise that reinforces your products or services. Depending on your field of business, a personal touch may work best. Whatever you choose, keep in mind that the more your name says, the less you will have to say and the less you will have to educate about your business. Use your business's name to fuel your marketing flight for the long haul, not just the short connection!

Mixing Rocket Fuel

Once you're confident you've got the right name for your business, then use it as a catalyst to create combustible fuel for your marketing momentum. Make sure your name makes sense with your logo, even if it's something as simple as the name of your business in a certain font and color. Your company's name and logo should be a central part of everything you do—from your business card, your storefront design, your interior décor, your website, and social media, to your advertising and promotional materials. Pay attention to these details because this is part of the message you want to convey to your customers: that you know what you're doing and can handle all the details involved in serving them and providing an excellent experience.

Once you have your company name and logo, use them in new and creative ways to ignite your rocket boosters and deliver your company's message. Like the name, your message should be simple, memorable, and distinct from your competition's message. If your company and your message remain aligned, then over time the two become virtually synonymous. Just consider a few examples:

Allstate Insurance: You're in Good Hands
McDonald's: I'm Lovin' It
Nike: Just Do It
Kentucky Fried Chicken: Finger Lickin' Good
Burger King: Have It Your Way
eBay: Buy it. Sell it. Love it.
BMW: The Ultimate Driving Machine

What do each of these pairs have in common? They all convey a memorable message embedded in the name of the business or organization. Probably by the fourth or fifth time you read or heard the message, you could repeat it yourself. These messages are not only easy to remember, they also tell us something about the company. You have only a few seconds to impress the customer *and* get your message across. So make it simple, but something that will stand out. If you rely on "Sherry's Shoes: In Business Since 2000" or "Clyde's Car Detailing: Your Local Specialists," then you're wasting a huge and vitally important opportunity!

Once you've aligned your name brand and message, then use this combination like the powerful rocket fuel it can be. Use it on your promotional materials, use it in your advertising, on your business card, your giveaway items such as calendars and key chains—and most definitely have it on your website and social media pages! It's important once you have your message that you continue to use it as you reinforce your brand. Working hard to massage your message into the memory of everyone you encounter will soon create a contagious combustion of public awareness.

Just Be-Cause

Once you have realigned all of your key pieces, then it's time to get creative and strategic in using them in synchronous ways. Most people use flyers, ad buys in radio or on TV, online banners, and Facebook comments. These messages usually tell the consumer *what* they have, but often fail at sharing *why* they should buy it. Strategic marketing isn't just about the "what" you have but also the "why." As entrepreneurial guru Seth Godin explains, "Marketing is no longer about the stuff that you make, but about the stories you tell."

What story are you telling with your marketing and messaging? Is this the best narrative to bring in new customers and to sustain the business you already have? What role does the customer have in your story? How can you engage customers *actively*?

Consider the experience you want to give people when they encounter your marketing and its messaging. How do you want them to feel? What felt-need do you want to spark inside them so that they will be drawn to what you're offering? Again, never forget that you're solving a problem for them in some meaningful way, whether it's by providing convenience, efficiency, quality, reliability, or some other combination of desirable feelings.

Never underestimate the power of fun to get your message out. Not so long ago the ALS Association garnered national attention by creating a brilliant gimmick that had everyone from kindergartners to Kardashians wanting to participate. The Ice Bucket Challenge swept the country and was everywhere, on TV and in the news and all over social media—and it didn't cost a dime! Their cause attracted support from people their budget could never have afforded, but because it was cause-driven marketing, many celebrities, athletes, and performers gladly participated and then posted, linked, and wrote about their experience.

Purpose-driven marketing is critical, particularly for nonprofit organizations. Just consider how breast cancer awareness has become synonymous with one color. And as a result, the Susan G. Komen Foundation has gotten big burly NFL football players to wear pink pants, caps, and gloves throughout the entire month of October! The foundation has been masterful in using cause-driven marketing. They understand that people like to get behind a worthy cause and back it as ambassadors spreading a message of awareness and support.

You don't have to be a nonprofit to utilize purpose-driven marketing. If you're committed to helping and enriching the lives of people in your community, you will automatically attract positive buzz about your business. I remember when I was growing up, it was often something as simple as having local businesses purchase uniforms for the kids' sports teams. Don't underestimate the impact of several dozen kids wearing the name of your business on their backs for months at a time! Professional sports teams know this trick as well and usually accept bids from corporate sponsors to name their stadiums.

Also, look for opportunities where you can support causes that naturally or logically relate to the kind of business you have. Maybe your baby boutique can sponsor a local marathon that promotes weight loss and wellness for new moms. Or your car repair shop might partner with Uber or another car service and offer free transportation on weekend nights in concentrated areas with lots of bars and clubs. It could simply be speaking at your local Toastmasters or civic club and providing tips for other small business owners and entrepreneurs.

Your cause-driven marketing effort might involve donating a certain amount of your products and services as part of the freebies given at fund-raisers or other cause-driven events. In return, you get your name listed and often prominently displayed at the event as well as allow potential new customers to sample your offerings. These opportunities can help expose your business to new sectors of your community, ones that you normally might not be able to reach.

Shrewd entrepreneurial marketers know it isn't enough to simply be good at something—if you get behind a cause, it can ignite a viral wildfire!

Who You Know

Never forget that marketing relies on relationships, not only with your customers but also with strategic partners who can help multiply your marketing efforts. My mother used to say success is not just about what you know—it's also about who you know! She understood that your entire network of relationships can be engaged to help you extend your brand and spread your message.

This kind of marketing might be as creative and relational as getting a rapper to wear your designer shoes. You might not have direct access to such celebrities or public figures, but someone in your network might be able to help you get their attention. This type of marketing franchises the influence of others to propel your product.

And nowadays you don't even need an introduction to contact most influential people. Using social media, you have direct access. I just read recently that some high school students contacted a famous NFL quarterback because their teacher, a huge fan of this player's team, said that if this player contacted her directly, the kids wouldn't have to take their final exam. Sure enough, the students went online and the football star responded to their request, contacted their teacher, and the teacher canceled their exam!

Sometimes you don't need a celebrity endorser to get your message out there. Instead, you need what Malcolm Gladwell calls "connectors" and "mavens" in his contemporary classic book *The Tipping Point*. According to him, connectors love networking, making introductions, and providing relational glue among the many people they know and encounter. These are the people you know who seem to know everyone else! Because they're often extroverted and gregarious, these connectors enjoy helping you meet other influential people.

Mavens differ from connectors, according to Gladwell, in that mavens provide information about various products, services, and businesses. These are your friends who love to go shopping with you because they know what's on sale at which stores. They naturally like to compare various businesses and find the ones with the best deals, the best products, and the best customer service. A maven who likes you and your company will naturally be directing more business your way.

Whatever you want to call them, people who know how to maximize their online presence are often invaluable marketing resources. In our global online community, simply having a strong online following can land you a role in a movie, a record deal, or a job as a news correspondent. You can launch a career as a singer, makeup artist, interior decorator, or model based on cultivating a large online fan base.

Because you never know who might be watching! You might have forgotten, but pop superstar Justin Bieber was discovered by Usher from a YouTube posting. This was also how the hip-hop artist known as Soulja Boy made it to the top of the Billboard Hot 100 in 2010 with his hit "Crank That." With a huge online fan base on MySpace and YouTube, this young artist from Chicago caught the eye of hip-hop producer Mr. Collipark, who signed him to Interscope Records. He reportedly earned more than $7 million that year, making him one of the highest-paid hip-hop artists of his generation (https://monetizepros .com/features/25-celebrities-who-got-rich-famous-on-youtube/).

Or consider how Whitney White has accumulated an incredible online presence since posting a profile video on her Naptural85 channel to commemorate going with a natural hairstyle. That initial video led to features on styling, best practices, and tutorials for other women interested in pursuing a similar look. Today she has more than a million followers thanks to YouTube, Facebook, Twitter, and Instagram (https://www.youtube.com/user/Naptural85/about).

I learned the value of leveraging online platforms firsthand. When I was doing my talk show, one of the things my producers and I discussed in choosing a guest often included how many You-Tube hits they got or how many Facebook friends they had. We understood that when these guests posted their visit on the show or mentioned appearing in my movie, we gained additional viewers or ticket sales we wouldn't normally have gotten. These influential online personalities helped us burn the bushel without adding to the budget!

As we conclude our exploration of the kinds of marketing that can take you to the next level, I hope you have been inspired to try new approaches and to initiate creative strategies. Just remember, great marketing doesn't depend on how much money you spend—it relies on consistent value in your messaging. Great marketing provides potential customers with an experience that establishes a relationship with you and your business. From that relationship, trust is born, which in turn leads to increased revenue for you.

Ultimately, the best marketing methods always return maximum exposure for minimum cost!

CHAPTER 12

New Frontiers

Creating Your Legacy

My legacy is that I stayed on course...from the beginning to the end, because I believed in something inside of me.

—Tina Turner

I will soon be celebrating the sixth decade of my life. In fact, by the time you read this, Lord willing, I will have passed this milestone birthday and entered into the next chapter of my life, my ministry, and my career as an entrepreneur. While I excitedly anticipate celebrating with my family and friends, I've made it clear to them that I better not receive any "over-the-hill" cards, black balloons, or funereal bouquets! Yes, this birthday is a special time to look back and savor the flavor of the many blessings in my life, to reflect and take inventory and revel in all that I have been privileged to accomplish in my time here on earth.

But it's also time to look ahead and ignite some new ventures! If you know me at all, then you know I'm not one to sit around and rest on my laurels and talk about the good old days! I've always looked to the future, anticipating the endless possibilities and potential points of power waiting just over the horizon, exploring creative opportunities not yet imagined as well as harvesting the fruition of what was once only instinct and intuition. I'm a firm believer that the best is yet to come—not just for me but for you as well!

Excuse Your Excuses

Whether you're sixteen or sixty, no matter where you may be in your season of life, you are uniquely equipped to bring your entrepreneurial vision to life, to grow it into a thriving success, and to leave a legacy of wisdom, wealth, and worth to those behind you. Whether you're a millennial just starting out and, like my son entering the music industry, want to be taken seriously, or whether you're a retired baby boomer wondering if you should dare to start a new venture at this age and stage, you have what it takes to soar. It's time to excuse your excuses and make some decisions that can change the rest of your life—and change the impact your business could have on your family for generations to come.

Too often I encounter people who have flirted with being an entrepreneur their entire life but have never risked taking action to ignite this aspect of their identity. They've remained on the sidelines, reading business books and attending conferences, brainstorming ideas and talking about possibilities with friends, watching *Shark Tank* and knowing more than the participants they see pitching new ideas to expert investors. But throughout the years, these individuals have remained on the edge of the runway, too afraid to risk redefining themselves, reinventing their careers, and redistributing the responsibilities in their lives.

If you are one of these people, then I exhort you to put this book down right now—okay, since we're on the last chapter, you can finish it first!—and take action today. Just take one step. Maybe it's looking at your finances and actually mapping out how much you could invest in a new business and what it would take to sustain your lifestyle for the first few years. Or it could be simply going to one of the many sites to register online domain names and checking to see if that business name that's been floating in your mind for months is available. Perhaps it's just having a conversation with someone you know at church who is doing what you wish you were doing.

After that first step today, begin making a list of steps you can take next and see which ones need to come before the others. Read back through this book and make notes about what resonates most with you and what requires further study and more research. Then create a draft of your business plan and ask at least two entrepreneurs you know and trust to critique it for you. Even if some steps seem out of order, the fact that you are taking action will lead you to get your dreams off the ground and in the air.

If you're one of those people who would tell me it's too late, that your ship has already sailed, then I strongly encourage you to reconsider your calendar. I encounter so many people, many at church, who have recently retired and act like their lives are already over. They assume that just because they're no longer going to work every day and the kids are grown, they might as well just sit outside the funeral parlor and wait their turn. They dress like housebound seniors in their eighties and nineties instead of the healthy hipsters in their fifties and sixties they could be.

Forgive me for exaggerating (only slightly, though) to make my point, but if you think it's too late for you to become an entrepreneur, then why are you still reading this book? Could it be that deep inside you know that you have what it takes if you only step out in faith? Could it be that you long to leave a legacy for your children and grandchildren so that their lives could be enriched by your ingenuity, innovation, and imagination?

If you're tempted to hide behind this excuse, then I pray you would reconsider your understanding of retirement. Just because you retire from one job or career doesn't mean that your life is over. It's like when we were in high school and we finally graduated. We had fulfilled the educational requirements for a major milestone in our lives, but I suspect you would never tell an eighteen-year-old, "Congratulations! But, sorry, your life is over." No! In fact, it's just the opposite—this ceremony is called "commencement" because it's the beginning of an entirely new chapter of life!

The same is true for you, my friend. Age and experience, when combined with action and enthusiasm, can make a powerful set of wings!

Legacy of Faith

In addition to experience and experimentation, you will also need faith if you want to leave a legacy that will enrich future genera-tions. Because the inheritance you leave for your family and loved ones consists not only of monetary and material possessions. It also consists of your courage, character, creativity, and combustibility—qualities that can influence the preferences and predispositions of your children and grandchildren as much as the code embedded in your DNA. If you model the kind of integrity, industry, and innova-tion that being a successful entrepreneur requires, you set a prec-edent that's more powerful than any royal privilege of ancient days.

In fact, you don't need to look any further than the lineage of Jesus to see the way his ancestors, both male and female, contrib-uted to his divine lineage here on earth. And just consider how many times these forefathers and mothers suffered disappointment, disaster, disease, and devastation. Women like Ruth and Rahab, who each watched God turn their risks into rewards. Men like Jacob and David, underdogs who fought their internal impulses as much as their external antagonists. Generation to generation, each persevered to provide more for their children and grandchildren, to leave more behind them than what they started with.

And it's not just the ancestors of Jesus—the Bible is filled with stories of men and women with entrepreneurial spirits who were rewarded for their faithfulness as God's stewards. In the New Testament book Hebrews, there is a who's who of the Bible that recounts what each individual overcame and what they are remembered for now. This passage begins by defining faith as "the substance of things hoped for, the evidence of things not seen" (Heb. 11:1 KJV). These two ingredients, *substance* of what you hoped for and *evidence* of what was once only a dream, provide a divine recipe for faith that extends beyond our religion, denomination, or place of worship.

Substance here literally means "to support" or "to hold up." It implies the way our faith supports who we are and all that we do in the same way a foundation supports a building. Without a strong foundation of faith, you would have given up your dreams a long time ago. But you haven't! You are still pursuing them and willing to hope for more as you now act on them.

Evidence as it's used in this verse means "conviction" or "concluding belief." Just as a scientist conducts experiments to test his hypothesis until he reaches a conclusion, we also rely on trial and error in the pursuit of our entrepreneurial dreams. Applied to our faith, evidence is our inward confidence in seeing God bless our endeavors and anoint our actions.

Give Your Best

Stressing his point that the only way to know God and enjoy his favor is by faith and faith alone, the writer of Hebrews then gives example after example of men and women who chose to follow God despite what human logic, common sense, and other people told them. He begins with Abel who is remembered for what he offered to God as an act of worship. Much like the three people tasked with investing their master's talents, Abel's story reminds us that we always give our best.

By bringing up Abel, I can't help but think the writer of Hebrews also wanted to remind us of how God redeemed a family situation that seemed beyond hope. You might recall that Adam and Eve had two sons, Cain and Abel. God asked both men to present Him with an offering of their harvests. Abel was a shepherd and gave his very best, fattest lambs. A farmer who tilled the soil, Cain, however, gave an offering that did not please God. Angry and jealous of his brother, Cain then murdered Abel.

As if leaving the Garden of Eden wasn't enough, Adam and Eve lost both of their children. But their story wasn't over yet! God blessed them with another son, Seth, who went on to extend their lineage and redeem the loss of his brothers. So even when you feel like you've lost your spark of what was once an entrepreneurial fire within, it's never too late to birth a new child, a Seth, who can carry your legacy forward. If you have faith, then God will meet you there and nourish the seeds of new dreams He has placed within you and bring them to fruition. But you must not give up!

The writer of Hebrews goes on to list many other famous men and women of the Old Testament, most of whom you will remember from Sunday school. But for our purposes as entrepreneurs, one stands out from the rest for the way he exercised his faith. While all of these saints of the past are commendable for various reasons, we're told Noah was remembered in this Faith Hall of Fame for his work. "By faith Noah, when warned about things not yet seen, in holy fear built an ark to save his family. By his faith he condemned the world and became heir of the righteousness that is in keeping with faith" (Heb. 11:7).

Noah, as you might remember, was asked to begin building an ark long before the rains came. He had to choose whether to trust God and take action to prepare for what was about to happen or whether to trust his senses and the perspectives of the people around him. Stepping out in faith, Noah chose to pick up his hammer and start building something that probably made no sense to anyone else—maybe not even to himself! But like the Wright brothers and other entrepreneurial pioneers, Noah acted on the dream he had been given and it saved his life. And not only his life, but also the lives of his family and ultimately the human race!

I'm convinced taking these steps of faith and moving forward with specific actions is often our greatest challenge as entrepreneurs. But you can't leave your faith out of your business plan! You must do the research and due diligence, you must plan and look at factual data, but at some point you have to trust that your wings will lift you off the ground. If we put together a Hall of Fame for great entrepreneurs, I guarantee that entrepreneurs such as Steve Jobs, Oprah Winfrey, George Washington Carver, Shonda Rhimes, Wilbur and Orville Wright, Mary Kay Ash, Thomas Edison, and Tyler Perry could each attest to the role that faith played in their ascent.

It may be tempting to ask God to help you start a new business and then wait for an investor to knock on your door, but that's not living by faith. That's living by folly because you're not doing your part in order for God to do His. You're going to need to put yourself out there and call those investors, set up meetings, prepare your presentation, and rehearse your pitch.

Even after you've established your business and seen it succeed, you can't leave a legacy for future generations by settling for less than God's best. You're going to have to continue taking risks, persevering through problems, working hard, and growing your business. Like Abel, you must continue giving your best. Like Noah, you're going to have to keep building your boat even when there's not a cloud in the sky.

If you want God to bless your efforts and transform your innovation into an inheritance, then you must keep the faith and do the work. This is where millennials and young adults may have to push through a sense of entitlement that tempts them to leapfrog over the hard work their parents did to provide them with the potential for more they're now actualizing. Building your legacy as an entrepreneur requires faith, and faith requires active participation. Like my mother buying property as a young wife and mother so she could support her family in future decades, you must look ahead to your future and do what it takes now to secure the legacy you want to leave later.

My Eye on You

In fact, your legacy is already a work in progress whether you realize it or not. And once again, it's not just how much profit you're making and depositing in your kids' savings accounts or grandkids' college funds—it's about what you're sharing of yourself, your experience, and your wisdom. At a leadership conference where I taught recently, I emphasized the concept of how, when you're running any kind of business, large or small, it's important to participate in the exchange of knowledge with an investment in people, particularly younger individuals who look to you for guidance.

This paying it forward goes beyond merely networking but provides a bridge from your present to your future. This is one of the most important things we can do to not only build our businesses but also to have a positive impact on our communities and future generations. In the Psalms, God tells David, "I will instruct you and teach you in the way which you shall go. I will counsel you with my eye on you" (Ps. 32:8 WEB). I suspect this is the kind of role model and teacher we are to be to those in our sphere of influence as well.

As you work to establish productive relationships that can help you build your business and help others at the same time, I encourage you to focus on three goals. The first one is that you should teach down. As you're beginning your business, you may ask yourself whom you can teach. But there is always someone who knows less than you, and you should teach what you know to someone who doesn't know it.

Second, you should teach best practices to peers in lateral relationships. Not only can you, of course, learn from them as well, but this connection to others flying at similar altitudes to your own also provides another advantage. Your peers are the ones who share the same blessings and burdens. They understand what you're going through. The networking, mentoring, and teaching you do with this group is invaluable because there are times when you may find it more difficult to fellowship with those who aren't quite in the same airspace.

There may be times when you need to vent or ask hard questions and only those who have walked in your shoes will understand and be able to provide answers, direction, and guidance. Reaching across will keep you focused, motivated, and encouraged to keep going after your goals. It will help stimulate ideas that can help you sustain, grow, and expand your business.

Finally, don't forget to look up as you invest in others and make deposits for your entrepreneurial legacy. Most of us don't want to look up to someone who is doing better than we are for several reasons. We may be intimidated by their success or wonder what in the world they could learn from us. But gleaning up will allow you to receive as you give. It will allow you to be filled with more information and knowledge and wisdom so that the cycle can continue. All you learn from gleaning up you can share as you reach across and teach down.

This sounds like such a simple concept, but it's essential if we're to have a transformative impact on our community and create an enduring legacy for our children. Teaching, reaching, and gleaning allow us to take part in each other's personal growth as well as entrepreneurial success. If we followed this concept in our community more diligently, we could close the circle of impoverished thinking that often lingers around us. We would be taking responsibility for our success and investing in the success of pioneers, artists, innovators, and entrepreneurs to come.

One for All

This concept is certainly not new. In fact, I think it's the reason why other cultural groups come to America and, without speaking even a word of English, can open businesses and thrive. Think about how this happens: a family leaves their native land where opportunities are severely limited and comes to America. The family's children go to school while the adults find work doing whatever will pay for food and rent.

Upon arrival, our fictional foreign family also makes contact with others in their cultural community, gleaning everything they can about this country and the business world here. In many cases, several families might even participate in a communal living situation. They live conservatively, saving as much money as they can, and within a few years of arriving, they're able to open their own business. Then, after a few more years, more family members come over, and by this time the family that was here first teaches down. Soon they open another business or multiple locations of the first, and the family begins to build true wealth, all working together for the betterment of themselves and generations to come.

They work as collaborators to create a legacy enjoyed by many branches of the same family tree. In the meantime, they continue to work within their community, teaching, reaching, and gleaning. And when they teach down, they go all the way down to their children. These families are not building their businesses for one generation; it is all about a legacy for them. They build their businesses with their children involved all the way. Rarely are their children even given a chance; they're brought into the business from the beginning. They learn the significance and fulfillment of hard work at an early age.

If the family owns a grocery store, the children are there bagging groceries. If they own a nail shop, the children are in there cleaning up and setting up for the next workday. If they own a dry cleaner, the children sort through the clothes and direct them to the appropriate type of cleaning. Through that work and the teaching from their parents and other older relatives, the children are becoming a part of the business. They're being handed the business every day of their life. This is what they do. They are always someone's teacher, but they are also, always, someone's student. This is the model that we have to recognize and learn how to use so that we can climb up as well.

I have spent a lot of time teaching down and reaching across because I enjoy both of those activities. What you may be surprised to know is that I glean up as well. We all have to glean up, because none of us has ever truly arrived. When I was getting ready to start my own talk show, Oprah, Dr. Phil, and Steve Harvey all reached out to me, letting me know that if I had any questions or needed anything, they were available to help. I was so grateful they reached out to me because the truth is I had already planned to glean up to them.

I want to glean from people who have already done what I want to do and who have done it well. I want to glean from people who are already where I want to be. I want their knowledge and their wisdom because anything they can teach me, anything I can learn will shorten my learning curve. So I will ask questions no matter how old I am, lots of them, and learn all that I can because I want to not only do well, I want to be ready for the next ones who will need me to reach down and teach them.

If this could become our community's mantra—teach, reach, and glean—I believe we could have a solid foundation of visionary entrepreneurs building a lasting legacy for generations to come!

Skywriting

Many times when people have approached me for advice or counsel on their entrepreneurial ventures, they lay out their business plan with startling clarity backed by solid, up-to-date sales data and marketing research. They answer each of my questions with a specific, thoughtful reply indicating careful forethought and deliberation. They have chosen an original, memorable name for their business and it is accompanied by clever slogans, logos, and branding material. They have secured their business website domain and lined up a web designer that fits their budget.

These individuals are like pilots sitting in their aircrafts on the runway. Their engines are running, their cargo has been safely stowed, and all cross-checks are complete. They have been cleared by the tower for takeoff, and yet they continue to sit, idling their engines and waiting for a certain sign. Often they have been praying about whether to start their business or asking God to reveal the right time for their launch.

After they have completed their description and answered my questions, I usually smile at them and ask, "How can I help you? It sounds like you're ready."

"Really?" they say. "So you think I should take the plunge and go for it?"

"I can't answer that question," I say. "Only you can. But if you're waiting on skywriting or some other sign to assure you that your business won't fail, falter, or flounder, then I'm afraid you will never get started. Risk is always part of the joy of being an entrepreneur—so embrace it!"

These words are not always the benedictory blessing they are looking for from me, but they are the best, most honest ones I can offer. So with every hope and prayer that your vision becomes a reality, I encourage you, too, to complete the groundwork, build your vision, and see it soar. There are no guarantees of success or secrets to ensure your venture gets off the ground and reaches the heights you want it to reach. You will probably not have the skywriting from God or anyone else you might like.

But I can promise you this: if you never take the risk to get your baby off the ground and fly, you will always live with regret. You will come to the end of your life wondering what happened to your vision, what the world would have looked like from 30,000 feet, wishing you had mustered the courage, like the Wright brothers and Daedalus and Icarus, to take flight.

As our journey across the skies of entrepreneurial success concludes, it seems only fitting to leave you with an urgent message that I borrow from one of the great advertising slogans of all time: *just do it*. Time is of the essence, my friend, and although it is never too late to get started, you do not want to waste any time in the present when you could be investing in your future. Do the hard work required to start your business, check the weather conditions and wind patterns, ask God to bless your efforts and give you guidance and wisdom, and then just do it!

You have the power within you to succeed beyond your wildest dreams. The sky is no limit to all that you can do with what God has given you. So catch a really big vision for what you can accomplish and stretch your talents and learn as you grow into the wings you've worked so hard to develop. Smile at the birds flying alongside you and kiss the clouds as you get ready see your vision reach heights you could have never imagined and as you discover all that waits ahead as you dare to soar. I hope to hear from you someday, perhaps at a conference or corporate event, when you approach and tell me that I played a small role in providing winds of encouragement beneath your wings of success. Until that moment, may God speed you on your journey.

It's no longer time to fly, my friend—it's time to soar!

Acknowledgments

No matter how independent, self-sufficient, or original you may be, you will never get your dreams off the ground and sustain flight without the assistance of numerous, equally talented individuals. Throughout my life I've been blessed by hundreds of people who have taught me, challenged me, and inspired me to explore new endeavors and blaze a trail all my own. I'm so grateful to the many thought leaders, entrepreneurs, CEOs, and elected officials who have pollinated my raw skills with their tremendous expertise by allowing me into their boardrooms and business environments. Without you, I would never have been able to get my flight plans to fruition!

Rolf Zettersten and his team, my publishing partners at Faith-Words, embraced the unique shape of *SOAR!* from the beginning and shared a vision bigger than either of us could have imagined when this book first took flight. Thank you to my editors, Joey Paul and Virginia Bhashkar, for their hard work and dedication throughout the process.

I'm indebted to my team at TDJ Enterprises, including my son Jamar Jakes for his many contributions that have allowed *SOAR!* to take off on schedule.

Dudley Delffs shared his wisdom on writing and brought his editorial expertise to the process of getting *SOAR!* off the ground. Thank you, Dudley, for flying with me on this one!

Jan Miller and Shannon Marven and their team at Dupree

Miller & Associates continue to copilot my publishing endeavors with energy, efficiency, and excitement. Their tireless efforts speak louder than words about their passionate investment in me and my mission.

Thank you, Jermaine, Jamar, Cora, Sarah, and Dexter for the privilege of seeing you leave the nest and take flight successfully into adulthood. I'm grateful for my acquired sons, Cora's husband, Brandon Coleman; and Sarah's husband, Touré Roberts. My wonderful wife, Serita, has flown by my side through all the ups and downs and has continued to provide her love, security, support, and serenity through them all. My love and thanks to you all.

And most important, to God be the glory for the things He has done!

Appendix

References and Resources

Starting a new business is a daunting task, no matter what size enterprise you want to create. Whether you're setting up a small boutique, baking pies out of your home, or dreaming of something larger, you want to establish your new venture correctly from the beginning. You can never have too much information or be too familiar with the basics of sound business practice, so I've created this section as a resource covering some of the nuts and bolts of business. This collection of definitions, references, and other resources is by no means comprehensive or definitive; it is simply my curated compilation intended to equip you with the basics of aerodynamic propulsion needed to get your business off the ground. I hope you find it useful and refer to it frequently.

Definition of Terms

Sole Proprietorship

A sole proprietorship is the simplest business model and, as its name implies, refers to a business owned and managed by only one person. The owner, or sole proprietor, is in direct control of all parts of the business and is also responsible for all the finances of the business, including any debt. Legally, in a sole proprietorship there is no difference between the business and the person. While the owner receives all the benefits of the business (income, profits, assets, as well as tax write-offs), the owner is also financially liable for any losses. For example, if the business owes any money, the owner's personal finances can be used to cover that debt.

Although the owner and the business are basically one entity, the business can have a different name. It often varies by state or region, but it's traditionally been known as "Doing Business As" or DBA. This filing allows you to use a fictitious name for your business that is different from your personal name and allows you to operate in all functions under this name, including getting a bank account for your business, an essential part of managing it successfully and keeping verifiable records.

Partnership

A partnership is a business that is owned by more than one person, with the division of assets and liabilities determined in the partnership agreement. The duties of each partner also have to be spelled out in the partnership agreement, as well as the financial responsibilities, so that both or all partners operate and perform under the same guidelines and consistent contractual understanding.

I'm a big believer in partnerships. Two or more people working together allow the business to leverage the strengths and skills of each partner to create a total greater than the sum. It's not just a cliché—two heads are better than one! With more knowledge, more experience, and more talent, the chances of success will always be exponentially greater.

Corporation

A corporation operates as a legal entity separate from the owners or the group of officers, often known collectively as a board of directors. The corporation has all the legal rights of an individual and can enter into contracts and other legal agreements, obtain credit, hire employees, and sue or be sued by another individual or corporate entity.

There are several types of corporation, with the most common being a C corporation, an S corporation, and an LLC (limited liability company). Each type of corporation has specific contextual advantages as well as limitations, and each carries distinct tax implications. In order to determine which corporate structure is best for you, do your homework and then consult a professional accountant, business attorney, or both. Don't encumber your business with more administrative layers than you need to operate effectively and efficiently.

Assets

Assets include all cash, cash equivalents (including accounts receivable), and property owned by a business. Products in inventory, office furniture, supplies such as computers, cell phones, and tablets are all assets, although over time they will not retain the value of what you paid for them. But all have value and can be liquidated at any point. These are considered tangible assets, items you can put your hands on, sell if needed, and immediately infuse cash into a business.

Most businesses have other, more intangible assets as well, including trademarks, patents, copyrights, intellectual properties. Over a period of sustained success, even the name of a business may become equitable and add financial value to a business and its worth.

Liabilities

The opposite of assets, liabilities refer to items in the negative column of the balance sheet and represent any debt for which the business is liable, which in turn reduces the company's net worth.

Liabilities often include credit cards, business loans, and outstanding bills that have to be paid to suppliers or other vendors. All taxes that have to be paid and any money owed to investors must also be considered liabilities.

Not all liabilities are current, meaning that some bills are due immediately (for example, the rent for your office space is due in full each month) as contrasted with long-term debt, such as a loan that is repaid over time.

Cash Flow

Cash flow refers to the amount of money flowing *in* and *out* of the business on a regular, often monthly or quarterly, basis. It's basically determined by subtracting immediate liabilities from liquid assets in order to calculate the remaining balance of available cash. Positive cash flow means that the money coming in is enough to cover expenses, debt, and reinvestment (in terms of marketing, promotion, or expansion) and also to set money aside and save to provide a buffer against future financial issues that may arise.

This point bears repeating: every business needs to have money in savings for the same reason that you keep money in a personal savings account. Unexpected expenses come up—maybe a machine breaks or your monthly revenues were less than projected. Or something positive may happen—a catering business may receive a larger than normal order and need additional money from savings to cover the additional costs to fill the order. Whatever the reason, every business must have some money set aside. Negative cash flow, of course, means just the opposite: the business is not bringing in enough money to cover expenses. Cash flow must be closely monitored because too many months of negative cash flow will deplete all your assets and resources, forcing you to terminate your present business operations.

Accounts Receivable

Accounts receivable refers to the amount of money your business is owed by your customers and clients. Many businesses do not have accounts receivables because the customers pay for the products they receive at the point of purchase. Many service businesses, however, such as day care centers, home health care agencies, and janitorial businesses bill monthly. In these situations, clients are typically given "net 30" terms, meaning they have thirty days to make the payment for the product or service received. This is money in the pipeline. Whenever paid, this cash flow into your business contributes to its overall health, both short-term and annual.

Bottom Line

I suspect we all know what this is! The bottom line is the amount of money the business has earned or lost during a specific amount of time, usually a month, quarter, or year. Most businesses analyze this on a monthly basis rather than week to week because many things can change in the short term of seven days. A thirty-day view, however, offers a fairly accurate measurement of how your business is performing month to month. This perspective usually provides a picture of trends such as which months are strongest, when revenues are trending up or trending down, and when expenses are trending up or trending down. These patterns and cycles help you understand whether your bottom line is strong or needs strengthening.

Financial Reports

The financial reports of the business give you a comprehensive account of everything that is going on within the business financially. There are several reports that you (or your accountant) should create and compile for your business regularly. These reports are usually required documents when seeking financing or presenting proposals to potential investors.

Even if you're building this business yourself with your own financing, it makes sense to do these reports regularly to have an understanding of the health of your business. After all, while you may not have any outside investors, *you* have invested. You are the stockholder and therefore should have an idea of how your investment is growing.

The three financial reports most crucial to monitoring the financial side of your business are:

1. BALANCE SHEET

The balance sheet is a financial statement indicating the bottom line, or big picture, of a business. It tells you what a business is worth (what the company owns and what it owes) over a specific period (monthly, quarterly, annually) and provides a snapshot of the business for that time frame. The balance sheet adds up the company's assets, its liabilities, and the capital of the business or the owner's equity.

This is called a balance sheet because the report has two columns and the two sides should balance each other. One side lists all the assets of the business and the other side lists the liabilities and the owner's equity.

Assets = Liabilities + Owner's Equity

2. PROFIT AND LOSS STATEMENT

This financial statement (also referred to as a P&L or Income Statement) takes a picture of projected sales and income compared to expenses (for the same period) to determine the net profit during that time. The formula for the Profit and Loss Statement typically looks like this:

Gross Profit – Total Operating Expenses = Net Profit

While most of the time Profit and Loss Statements are summarized quarterly or annually, some businesses may calculate P&Ls for a shorter duration. With certain businesses, projecting a P&L often makes sense for determining the viability of a certain event, product, or client. This may be the case for an event planner or a caterer. For example, an event planner trying to determine the profitability of a particular event would compare the **gross profit**, the amount of money the event planner will earn for putting together the event, with **total operating expenses**, the cost of putting on the event. This has to include all costs the event planner will incur, such as the rental of the venue (if the planner is covering that), the employees' salaries for the additional servers who will be used for the event, all costs for the food and drink, the costs for any music or other entertainment, the cost of travel, and any other expenses that the event planner has to cover, and so on. The difference between the gross profit and the total operating expenses determines the **net profit** (or **net loss**).

For an event planner, this P&L can determine if a particular job is profitable enough to accept. Doing a P&L over a longer period of time and then comparing the current P&L with previous ones will highlight any changes in your business and could show potential areas of concern. For example, you may see that your income or gross profit is growing but your expenses are increasing at an even greater rate or percentage. When you see these kinds of red flags, you can analyze the steps you can take.

3. CASH FLOW STATEMENT

This statement highlights how much money is coming into the business and how much money is going out of the business. What is coming in includes all sales: cash, credit cards, accounts receivable. What is going out includes all credit and debt expenses, salaries, taxes, as well as loans or any other expenses that must be paid. This statement will help you answer this most important of questions: can I stay in business at this ratio? In other words, can you sustain flight at this altitude knowing the amount of fuel required to fly that high? Cash flow statements show the liquidity of the company.

Other Resources

We are fortunate to live at time when there is an abundant wealth of resources to educate, stimulate, and accelerate entrepreneurs. Here are some of my favorites to get you started. Depending on your needs and the kind of business you wish to launch, do as much online research as possible to utilize the resources most pertinent for you.

1. **Small Business Association** (www.sba.gov) is far more than a lending resource. The SBA is an independent agency that aids, counsels, assists, and protects the interests of small businesses. From providing resource guides to workshops and tool kits to help you start your business, the SBA is a valuable resource for every small business.

2. **National Association of the Self-Employed** (www.nase.org) is the largest nonprofit, nonpartisan business association in the country. It provides small business owners with the everyday support most entrepreneurs need, including access to experts, educational benefits and resources, information on funding, and the privileges and buying power of a large organization. Information on their website will also keep you up to date with any imminent changes that could affect your business. And there is a funding part of the organization as well. It is the largest nonprofit, nonpartisan association in the country.

3. **National Federation of Independent Business** (www.nfib .com) is a network of more than 300,000 independent business owners in all fifty states and Washington, DC. Their mission statement: "To promote and protect your right to own, operate and grow your business." It is the leading advocacy group for small business owners, and in addition to their advocacy they offer business products and services for small businesses at discounted rates.

4. **Score** (www.score.org) is a mentor-matching program where new business owners are paired up with volunteer mentors who have a wealth of information and years of experience.

5. **LivePlan** (www.liveplan.com) offers business plan software to assist you in putting your plan together. Many different types of software are available for constructing your business plan. If LivePlan isn't viable for your purposes, then keep searching for the right software for your venture.

6. **Small Business Trends** (www.smallbiztrends.com) is an award-winning online publication for small business owners with articles that help you take your business to the next level. With articles and ideas on how to use technology, maximize marketing, build your brand, and handle financial situations, this is an invaluable resource for your ongoing entrepreneurial education.

7. **Entrepreneur** (www.entrepreneur.com) offers both a print and digital magazine that provides small business owners with ideas, advice, inspiration, and strategies to help grow your business.

8. **Black Enterprise** (www.blackenterprise.com) first began as a premier business news and investment resource for African Americans, but now the magazine and website have grown to

be so much more. The BlackEnterprise.com website delivers all the information and inspirational stories the magazine has been providing since 1970 (and still does). While the magazine is monthly, the website is updated constantly, so you should check it frequently for the latest news and resources for your business interests.

About the Author

T. D. JAKES is a #1 *New York Times* bestselling author of more than forty books and is the CEO of TDJ enterprises, LLP. He is the founder of the thirty-thousand-member Potter's Houses Church and his television ministry program, *The Potter's Touch*, is watched by 3.3 million viewers every week. He has produced Grammy Award–winning music and such films as *Heaven Is for Real, Miracles from Heaven*, and *Jumping the Broom*. A master communicator, he hosts MegaFest; Woman, Thou Art Loosed! and other conferences attended by tens of thousands. T. D. Jakes live in Dallas with his wife and five children. Visit www.tdjakes.com.